BEN

All profits from the sale of this book will go to the Ben Hardwick Memorial Fund

Photographs © BBC by Les Wilson, Topical Production Unit, Lime Grove.

Published by the British Broadcasting Corporation,
35 Marylebone High Street, London W1M 4AA

ISBN 0 563 20331 5

First published 1985

© Esther Rantzen and Shaun Woodward 1985

Typeset in 11/13pt Linotron Plantin by Phoenix Photosetting, Chatham
Printed in Great Britain by Mackays of Chatham Limited

BEN
THE STORY OF BEN HARDWICK

ESTHER RANTZEN AND SHAUN WOODWARD

Photographs by Les Wilson

British Broadcasting Corporation

Acknowledgements

We would particularly like to thank Professor Roy Calne, Celia Wight and other members of the surgical and medical team at Addenbrooke's Hospital in Cambridge.

We would also like to thank the staff at the liver transplant unit at King's College Hospital, especially Professor Roger Williams, Professor Eric Stroud, and Dr Alec Mowatt. Dr Jardine at Queen's Medical Centre in Nottingham, as well as other medical staff at the hospital, helped us enormously in telling this story.

We would like to thank all the *That's Life* team, particularly Catherine Boyd, Gillian Bradley, Tony Chapman, Alison Eisberg, Bob Marsland, Martin O'Collins, John Pettman, Bryher Scudamore, Andy Stevens, Gordon Watts and Les Wilson.

In America we would like to thank Todd McNeely and his parents Stephen and Linda, as well as other members of the Children's Liver Foundation. We would like to thank Professor Tom Starzl and other members of his surgical team at the University of Pittsburgh.

In preparing this book we are grateful for the help which Susan Kennedy has given. Other friends have been very kind in the help and encouragement they have offered, particularly Richard Ballantine and Desmond Wilcox.

Without the help of the *That's Life* viewers this story could never have taken place. To all those who gave money and support we are very grateful, especially two individuals who are very much a part of this story, but who wish to remain anonymous. Without their generosity and humanity this story and its achievements might not have been so successfully realised.

Above all, our thanks go to the families whose story we tell in this book. Their courage and devotion led to unprecedented achievements in transplantation, and have saved many lives.

For Matthew and Ben

CHAPTER ONE

This is the story of a very special child. Not a famous child, the son of a prince or a prime minister. But an ordinary two-year-old boy, Ben Hardwick, whose example has led to the saving of many hundreds of other lives we will never hear about.

Tragically, Ben Hardwick himself could not be saved. He was desperately ill when this story begins, and according to his doctors, had only a few weeks left to live. His only chance was a liver transplant, but children who need liver transplants must have child donors, and at that time child donors could not be found.

When Ben's story was told on television a donor was found. He had his transplant, and because of him, more donors have come forward, and more and more children are being saved.

But Ben himself was only given one more year of life. A cruelly short reprieve, and yet every extra day of a child's life is precious, to those who love him. Millions of people in this country loved Ben – for them that year was immeasurably precious. As one wrote to his parents, 'Ben was a lovely child, and everyone who saw him, loved him. When he smiled he really did make the whole nation smile with him. The memory of Ben will never leave us – the memory of that happy little face.'

And Ben achieved a miracle in that last year. He changed our attitudes, he created a breakthrough in transplant surgery. Ben made us realise that organ donation can save lives, can ease the suffering of thousands of people, adults and children, who undergo constant dialysis for chronic kidney failure. Transplants can restore sight to the blind, rescue from death those who would succumb to heart and lung failure, and yet the desperate need for donors was almost unrecognised until Ben's story was told.

The miracle was achieved through the courage and determination of Ben's parents, the compassion of bereaved parents like Mr and Mrs Fewkes, the dedicated brilliance of the transplant team at Addenbrooke's Hospital in Cambridge, under Professor Roy Calne, and with the help of a television programme.

The story begins in January 1984, in an office at the BBC. You might imagine a room thickly carpeted to hush the chatter of tele-printers, many television screens reflecting news bulletins from round the world. Incredibly beautiful secretaries weaving their way from desk to desk bringing urgent messages from viewers, and the occasional lightly shaken cocktail. That's the way we imagine it too, sometimes, say at 9.30 in the morning when some bureaucratic mandarin decrees that a man with a drill should start blasting the walls next to us so that we can't hear ourselves think, let alone a telephone ring.

In fact, we work in a slum. Lime Grove studios have known glamorous days, when they were the headquarters of Gainsborough Films and Jessie Matthews twirled across polished floors. Not much is polished there now, except the details of the young film director's expenses. It is run-down and dingy, and perhaps the dingiest corner of all is the *That's Life* office.

We who work on *That's Life* have our theories about the reasons why we are condemned to the most hideous offices in the BBC. One is that the BBC can't afford to improve the office. Another is that glossy offices make bad programmes. Most of the best programmes seem to have been made in caravans, or prefabs, or slums like ours. As we write, the *That's Life* team has been moved to a much bigger, more glamorous room. But don't worry – in three weeks we can turn this into a slum, too.

The slum is created because every week, while the programme is in production, we receive thousands of letters – up to 15,000 letters a week. The letters contain news clippings, photographs, peculiarly shaped vegetables, someone's faulty underwear, someone else's complicated life insurance. Somehow all this stuff has to be read, replied to, and returned, or filed. Two huge bins are soon full to overflowing with letters, read and unread.

In 1984 the programme had been on the air for eleven years, and was still one of the most popular programmes on British television, watched by around fourteen million people every week. Those overflowing letter-bins contain the secret of its success – hilarious stories taken from our viewers' lives, or desperately serious stories of injustices they have experienced. We are their last resort – they come to us because they know we reach the widest possible audience.

That's Life provides an audience of millions for the single voice – one individual member of our audience, whose story we tell. It's a peculiar programme – the staff work themselves to death on it, six days a week, twelve hours a day, at its worst. We believe our commitment to serve our viewers well, to deserve the trust they place in us, shines from the screen. We hope so, anyway. So, on that Wednesday afternoon in January, when Debbie Hardwick rang us, we were exactly the right programme for her message. She was telling us the story of her dying little boy – we could bring his tragedy to the widest possible audience. And perhaps that way we could save other children, even if we couldn't save Ben himself.

We had started this new series of *That's Life* the week before – it runs for six months, and always begins in those cheerless dark days after Christmas when we have nothing to look forward to but the fogs and snows of February. The first programme had been a good one, we felt. A very strong story about a deaf-blind girl wrongly diagnosed as mentally handicapped, a vicar complaining in plain-song that no one could find his church, a film of a toddler who played champion snooker. It may sound an eccentric combination, but the programme has always thrived on just this kind of unpre-dictable recipe.

At the production meeting on Tuesday morning, Esther as usual read out some of the letters in the 'goody box' – the collection of letters that the researchers had selected as being the most suitable for the programme. The programme editor, Gordon Watts, smiled his agreement at most of the ideas – occasionally voiced an objection. Soon everybody had a handful of strong stories to research.

Over the years we have established a research routine. The first step is to discuss the story thoroughly at the production meeting. At that stage everybody can contribute ideas from their own experi-ence, or from stories they have researched which may be relevant. It's an informal meeting, full of anecdote and laughter. It is where the items that will eventually make the programme are first discussed, and everybody sorts out at this meeting our reason for selecting a story, and how we intend to treat it.

But, of course, not all stories reach us in time for the production meeting. This week the meeting ended, and we all dashed to the canteen before it closed, fondly believing we had the basis of another good programme – but nothing out of the ordinary.

The next afternoon, Debbie rang us. The well-planned programme went out of the window. We found ourselves, as Esther later said to Shaun, holding a story so big it was like clinging on to the tail of an elephant, being swung about and buffeted by it, but still somehow keeping a grip on it. When everything was happening thick and fast, Esther yelled at Shaun, 'Make sure you keep a diary of all this.' 'Don't worry,' he said, 'I'm keeping one.'

Most of this book, and the extraordinary story it tells, is based on Shaun's diary.

SHAUN'S DIARY

Wednesday 11th January

Midday. I am working on the response to the item I had researched for last week's programme, about Dawn, the deaf-blind girl. Already offers of help are coming in. I am impressed by the way people seem to care, to want to help. Gill Bradley, one of the production assistants, interrupts me. There is a woman on the phone with a story Gill thinks I should hear. If Gill had been less interested, if she had just told the woman automatically to 'write in, please', perhaps this story would have ended here. But Gill has recognised the urgency in the woman's voice, and the desperation. I stop what I am doing.

The caller is Debbie Hardwick. She has spent the previous two days trying to decide whether or not to ring *That's Life* to see if we can help. This morning she has decided she has nothing to lose. She has rung the BBC switchboard and asked for the programme. Gill has picked up the phone.

Debbie asks whether we broadcast television appeals. Gill tells her not normally, but what is the problem? Debbie says that her little boy has hardly any time left to live, he needs a special operation which is not possible in Britain, even though the skills and techniques are available here. Sadly, what is not available is public co-operation and good will.

Gill refers the call to me. Debbie outlines her story. Her only child, Ben, was born with a liver disease, biliary atresia. Although he'd had two operations before he was even twelve months old, they'd failed to arrest the disease. The doctors have told Debbie that unless Ben can have a liver transplant before he is two, he will die. I ask her how old he is now. She says he was two last December.

Ben is now living on borrowed time. If he is to have any chance of living more than a few more weeks, he needs a liver transplant now. I say that I didn't realise you could transplant a liver. Debbie says no, people don't know about it – even doctors in this country don't realise it's possible for a child – it's a new operation.

She explains that the operation has been successfully carried out on children like Ben, in America. One was a two-year-old who is now five, and doing very well. He'd had the same disease as Ben. The surgeons had said, when he had his transplant, that if they'd waited a few more weeks he wouldn't have been well enough to have the operation. And that's what the doctors are now saying about Ben.

At Addenbrooke's Hospital in Cambridge a surgeon, Professor Roy Calne, has successfully carried out liver transplants on adults. He saw Ben a few months ago and told Debbie that there is no surgical reason why Ben can't have the operation. But because it is impossible to obtain paediatric livers for children in this country, the operation can't be done. Ben, he told her, is certain to die.

Ben needs a liver from a child his own age or slightly older, no more than seven or eight years old. Of course, tragically, some children die every day in this country whose livers would be suitable for the operation, but doctors and paediatricians are too afraid, or upset, to ask the parents of a child who has just died if they can remove the liver. Ben will die because no one can actually bear to ask another parent to make the operation possible, and save his life.

I ask Debbie how she thinks we can help. 'Tell people that transplants are possible, if there are donors,' she replies. 'Please help me give him this chance. He's going to die if he doesn't get it. And even if Ben has to die, if it's too late for him, at least we may save other children in the future.'

11

As Debbie speaks, I find myself listening with the kind of intensity I might imagine listening to a judge passing a death sentence. She stops talking. What can I say? I explain that I'll have to think about what we might be able to do. I need to talk to Esther, and then I'll call her back as soon as I can.

At the time Esther is engaged in a conversation with the programme editor, Gordon Watts. I can hear lots of discussion about budgets and overspending. A bad time to interrupt. I interrupt. Rebuffed – she tells me we'll talk over lunch.

To get to the BBC canteen you have to walk along a labyrinth of corridors and staircases – even the minotaur would get lost in Lime Grove. My mind is travelling in its own labyrinth – much as I want to do something for the little boy, I can't see what we can do – not in just a few days, and that might be all the time he has left.

Esther suddenly breaks my concentration. Tray in hand – several cups of tea plus statutory meat and two veg – she sits down opposite me. You wanted a word, she says. Yes – and I tell her about the phone call. Esther sits, transfixed. Then bursts into a short, sharp speech.

'Film him. Now. Why are you eating lunch? You should have been halfway there by now. Get yourself a film crew – find a director and go. Of course we can do it.' I am already on my way out of the canteen, but not too far out of earshot to hear her remarking to a colleague, 'We can, can't we?'

Half an hour later I am still at Lime Grove. Esther walks into the office and asked why the hell we are still in the building. There is only one film director available, Tony Chapman, I say, and he doesn't think there's time to get to Chessington in Surrey, and back by 5.30 – the time the crew need to be back at their base in Ealing. 'If we stay here discussing you'll lose any chance of filming anyway. Just go. Go!'

We go. All the way to the car the film director keeps telling me why we shouldn't be doing it this afternoon. It's rushing things, he says. We can do it tomorrow; we'll have all day then, and we can get perfect shots. Why does she insist we do it today, he asks. Because Ben might just not be here tomorrow, I reply.

Every minute in the car seems to matter. I curse traffic lights that turn red as we approach. As we get nearer and nearer the house I

12

find myself wondering what are we going to find. Until now I haven't really thought about what he will look like. If he is so near to death, perhaps he'll be very feeble, very sickly and – this is television – very unappealing.

Then I begin to think about the questions I can ask his mother. Although I've been a researcher for two years on *That's Life*, used to asking questions, it's very different when the film cameras are rolling. Particularly when the subject, a dying child, is so very sensitive. I don't want to hurt Debbie, but I must encourage her to speak out.

We are there. Niven, our driver, wishes me good luck. As I climb the few steps to their front door, my mind rejects all thought of the framework of the interview and speculates wildly once again about what Ben will look like.

He is beautiful. Debbie answers the door, her little boy clinging desperately to her neck, saying 'Mum, Mum.' He is not at all sickly. Not feeble. He is like any other two-year-old. His tummy is slightly enlarged and his face is yellowy. But nothing indicates that this is a child who is about to die, that these are his last days. For a moment I do a double-take. Perhaps this isn't Ben? Perhaps it's the child of a friend that Debbie is minding for the afternoon. But it *is* Ben. This gorgeous blond blue-eyed boy who seems so normal is the boy who is certain to die.

Film crews have been everywhere, heard everything – it's their job. But after just a few minutes in Debbie's flat, with Ben and his mum together, the film director, cameraman, sound engineer, sparks and I have all been moved to tears as we listen to the story of Ben's short life in Debbie's simple, painful words.

Ben was born on 6th December 1981 in Chessington. Debbie was just 20. Ben was her first baby. When he was born, Ben had what seemed to be a cold. And, like so many other babies, he was jaundiced. No one was particularly worried about the jaundice since it is a common trait. A few days after he was born, Ben was allowed home. But he was soon back in hospital.

His jaundice had failed to clear up. Just two months after he was born he was admitted to King's College Hospital in London for tests on his liver. On 11th February 1982 Ben underwent major surgery. This revealed that he had biliary atresia – a condition which creates a blockage in his liver so that it cannot function. To clear the blockage and to reconstruct the tubes which carry the bile from the liver to the stomach a procedure – called a kasai operation – was necessary. If it worked, he might be able to lead a normal healthy life. If it failed he would probably die before he ever got to playschool.

After the operation Ben was allowed home. Time alone would tell whether it had worked. A year later the doctors told Debbie that the operation had failed. Ben was going to die.

She asked the doctors how much time he had left. It was impossible to say. He was already fifteen months old. He might just reach his second birthday in December if he was very lucky.

Debbie took Ben home. Where many people might despair, she couldn't give up hope. Yet no one was encouraging her to hope for anything. All the doctors could tell her was that there was nothing anyone could do to save his life. But Debbie went on hoping. One morning, waiting in the doctor's surgery, she picked up a copy of *Reader's Digest*. In the middle of the March edition was a story entitled 'Small Miracle for Todd McNeely'. Debbie read it:

> The only hope for the dying boy was a liver transplant – a procedure so risky only one pioneering US surgeon was willing to try it.
>
> 'Don't do it' paediatricians warned 31-year-old Linda McNeely. Liver transplantation they insisted was too risky. But in the spring of 1980 Linda and her husband, Stephen, a 33-year-old oil company executive, decided that they could not sit by and watch their only child die without a fight. . . .

The article said that a liver transplant had been the McNeelys' only hope. They got one. That was three years ago and Todd was now five and very well. From that moment the goal of a liver transplant for Ben became the force that kept Debbie going. Like the mother she'd read about in *Reader's Digest*, she decided that she could not sit by and watch her only child die without a fight.

Debbie wrote to Linda McNeely in America. In reply, Linda described how well Todd was now and she told Debbie that a surgeon called Professor Tom Starzl had performed the transplant operations in Pittsburgh, a town in central North America. But Linda went on to ask Debbie why she hadn't contacted a surgeon in England who carried out the same kind of liver transplants, Professor Roy Calne at New Addenbrooke's Hospital in Cambridge.

Debbie was absolutely stunned by Linda's letter. How could it have happened that no one in England, not *one* of the innumerable doctors she had seen, including specialists at King's College Hospital, the leading unit for children with liver disease, had even mentioned that liver transplants were being done here in this country. And that the surgeon who performed these miracle operations was based less than seventy miles away from Ben's home in London? Debbie was devastated and furious.

She wrote to Professor Calne immediately. Would he see Ben as soon as possible? Could Professor Calne give Ben a liver transplant? He responded straightaway: in his letter he explained:

> It is virtually impossible to obtain livers of the right size in the United Kingdom to transplant into children. We are therefore unable to offer a realistic chance of liver transplantation in the paediatric age group . . . I think it is really up to public opinion and the paediatricians to come to terms with providing donors for children in the same way that donors are found for adults with liver disease. I am sorry not to be more encouraging.

The letter came like a thunderbolt – for a few days all Debbie's hopes were crushed once again. Her mind turned to America. What if she could get Ben there? But how could she possibly manage to get the money together? Find the surgeons? Arrange the hospital? It seemed impossible.

Then, just as Debbie began to muster her hopes, Ben became desperately ill. He had septicaemia and went into a liver coma. In hospital doctors thought he would die within a few days. But Ben fought back and recovered. Debbie was able to take him home again.

It was Ben's strength which gave Debbie the courage to go on fighting. How could she give up while he was fighting so hard himself? From that moment, she began to call him 'my little soldier'.

Debbie contacted Professor Calne once again at Addenbrooke's. It was December. Ben would shortly be two – time was running out. Would Calne see him? Tell her how long he had and advise her how to go about getting help? Calne agreed to see Ben, and Debbie and her 'little soldier' travelled up to Cambridge.

There Professor Calne explained to Debbie that although not all children die as young as Ben from biliary atresia, his condition was terminal. A transplant would be Ben's only chance. Professor Calne estimated that about twenty-five children a year die from this disease who could be saved by a transplant. But no livers small enough for children were ever offered for transplant. He told Debbie he was sorry, but there was nothing more he could do. He had the expertise to perform the operation. Since 1968 he had carried out 150 liver transplants on adults. Thanks to a new 'miracle' drug, cyclosporin, to combat rejection, the success rate was now nearly 80 per cent. But nothing affected the death sentence he handed Debbie. There were still no donors for children. They could only die.

Nevertheless, he said, Ben's name would be put on a computerised waiting list called UK Transplant, the national organ-matching service. It was originally set up to match donors and recipients for kidney transplants. Vital details, blood groups and so on, of the desperately ill people hoping for a transplant are stored on a computer, always available the instant a donor is found. UK Transplant now stores details not just of kidney patients, but all sorts of patients needing transplants, including heart and liver. Professor Calne explained that, tragically, the waiting list was always lengthening and Ben's chance of help was infinitesimal. But he would make sure the little boy's vital medical information was recorded on the computer – just in case.

Debbie told Professor Calne that she would do anything to give Ben the chance to live. Calne explained that so, too, would dozens of other parents who every year go through the daily agony she was now enduring. Their babies, too, could be saved if paediatricians and doctors in intensive care units could bring themselves to discuss organ donation with other bereaved parents. By becoming a donor, one child, doomed to die, might save another child from dying. But doctors couldn't even suggest it – they found it too pain-

16

ful. They couldn't believe the idea might even comfort bereaved parents.

'I believe some parents would welcome the idea, if it were put to them,' Professor Calne told Debbie. 'At the moment, it's not. And to change doctors' attitudes would take a complete shift in public opinion. That is what you would have to achieve. You would have to marshal public opinion on your side.'

'How?' said Debbie.

'I suppose the first step would be to find yourself a friendly television producer,' he said. There was an irony in this advice. Just a few years ago, a *Panorama* programme about 'brain death', based on American cases, had frightened viewers so much that the number of donors dropped dramatically. Many doctors had become embittered about the kind of damage television could do to their work, particularly doctors working in the transplant field. Professor Calne responded differently. If one programme could swing public opinion away from organ donation, perhaps another could swing it back.

Debbie brought Ben back home with her to Chessington, every word Calne had told her engraved on her heart. He was Ben's only possible gateway to life. She followed his advice to the letter. She knew a man who worked in television, as a technician. She asked him whom she should contact. He suggested one of the afternoon programmes, or *That's Life*. The afternoon programme was polite, kindly, and asked her to write to them. *That's Life* sent a film crew down to see her, that very afternoon.

All the time Debbie is talking to me, I take notes. This is the information we'll need for the script on Sunday. She gives me the sheaf of letters between herself and Calne and herself and the American family. But if we are to change public opinion, Esther has left me in no doubt that we will need Debbie and Ben on film, to make the point. I needn't have worried. We start the interview.

Debbie has lived with this tragedy for nearly a year. The thoughts and feelings she describes have crystallised over the months. By now she is quite calm as she tells me that every day she wonders if this will be Ben's last. She dare not tell Ben off, like any other mother with a high-spirited two-year-old. Because, as she puts him to bed every night, she wonders to herself, is this the last time? Will he get up in the morning? He could just die tomorrow.

I ask the most important question. Is there a way she can put across to any bereaved parents the idea that doctors themselves can't put into words? Is organ donation perhaps an intolerable suggestion to make to parents, at a moment of intolerable tragedy? Debbie says, 'Surely, though, if that child has died, if that child has then given life to another child, isn't it some sort of consolation to the parents, eventually? Maybe not immediately. But eventually it must be some consolation that they have saved another child.'

As if he understands exactly what is happening around him, Ben, sitting on her lap, turns and looks up at her. He pulls her face down towards him. 'Mum', he whispers, 'Mum, Mum.' Perhaps he just wants a cuddle. But it sounds as if he is begging her to save him, somehow.

Silence fills the room. It's Ben who, a few seconds later, breaks the stillness. 'Bubbles, bubbles,' he says. I ask Debbie what he means. She says he wants his bath, which he loves filling with bubbles.

The film crew move into the tiny bathroom in the Hardwicks' flat. Tony Chapman directs a sequence which is to become a regular part of news bulletins during the next few months. Ben balances bubbles on his fingers, his huge blue eyes shining with happiness.

Debbie carefully bathes Ben as he splashes and blows bubbles into the air. She tells me that he is now being kept alive on a cocktail of nine different kinds of drugs every day. Without these drugs he would have died months ago. I can't help but wonder if people might think that such a huge operation on his tiny body would be an intolerable ordeal for him. That with no real chance anyway of getting for him the operation he needs, it might be better not to attempt to prolong his life. But then I look at him again and know that any view like this is completely untenable. Debbie tells me, 'Because he's such a happy child, you never hear him cry, so on occasions when he's not very well, and he really cries, it's very frightening. Because you think, "Is this it? Am I going to lose him?"'

18

CHAPTER TWO

The next morning, the office is filled with amiable chaos, as usual. A balloon manufacturer has rung in with the offer of a giant inflatable vicar to fly over the church nobody can otherwise find. We decide to inflate it and see if the congregation swells, too. A con man we have been tracking for six months has surfaced, and one of our viewers has alerted the police. There might be some way of referring to the arrest in the next programme – on the other hand, we could be breaking laws of contempt and get ourselves slapped into jail next to him. Tony Chapman, one of the film directors, is planning our next round of street interviews, but he grins at Esther when she asks how he thinks the filming with Ben had gone the day before. 'I think you'll like it,' he says.

Film is processed overnight. The sound is separately transferred from sound tape to film stock, and sound and picture have to be matched and synchronised by the film editors. The interview with Debbie will be ready to view around noon.

Esther reports the events of the previous day to Gordon Watts. He agrees it sounds a very strong story. 'I sent them off to film as fast as possible', she explains, 'because it sounds as if the little boy is running out of time. But obviously if the film is too painful, if he looks too ill, we may not be able to use it.' We decide to send our stills photographer, Les Wilson, a huge, gentle cockney, hung about with macho zoom lenses, because the effect on the screen of still shots can sometimes be kinder than the rawness of film.

At noon, Esther arrives in the cutting-room. The film editor, Christine Pancott, has another film ready for viewing on the screen. 'Have a look at this one first,' she suggests. 'Annie's nearly finished synching up yesterday's stuff.' Annie Terrell, Christine's assistant, is still whirling yards of film through her synchronising machine. 'How does Ben look?' Esther asks. 'Gorgeous,' Annie says. That is the main hurdle crossed. If Ben looks appealing, the point of his story will come home with even more impact.

Esther and Christine watch the other film, the team gallantly jumping round a holiday camp in the rain, trying to persuade the holidaymakers to join in an improvised version of 'I do like to be beside the seaside'. Christine has cut the music together brilliantly – the atmosphere is funny and jolly. Particularly when one lady leaps up and down to the music in synchronisation with her own bust. We agree the film is ready to show Gordon to see if he approves.

Then the spools of Ben's rushes are laced up, and Esther switches the machine to 'go'. There on the screen is the picture of an extraordinarily beautiful girl. Cameras are choosy, as we all know. Some lovely faces are completely unphotogenic. But the camera turns Debbie Hardwick into an outstanding beauty. It is enhanced by the way she explains her battle to save Ben. In every answer she seems to pick the perfect words to convey her emotion – but always calmly. Then come the pictures of Ben playing with his toy car. Then the heart-stopping sequence of Ben in the bath, with the bubbles, naked, vulnerable, happy. It is intolerable to think that that happiness would be so brief. And, most moving of all, the moment that sums up Debbie's hopelessness – when her son reached imploringly up to her, and seemed to beg for help, 'Mum, Mum, Mum.'

Esther switches off the machine. 'That has to be the last shot – it says it all,' she says. She's made notes through the viewing – she and Christine rapidly go through them together. Then Esther almost runs back to the office, to report to Gordon. She doesn't want to oversell it, in case he is disappointed when he sees the film. But she has to tell him how strong it is. 'They've done a good job,' she says. 'It's everything we'd hoped for, and more. It'll be ready for you to see first thing tomorrow.'

She goes over to Shaun's desk. 'It's amazing,' she says. 'Incredibly moving.' 'You mean I did something right?' says Shaun. 'I didn't notice you,' Esther says. 'Just Debbie and Ben.' Researchers need to be kept in their place. But he is right. He had been sensitive and perceptive, allowing Debbie to relax in the knowledge that the team genuinely cared about her, and her little boy. But there is no time to allow Shaun to preen himself. 'Have you checked it all out, what does Professor Calne say, have you spoken to America?' Under the onslaught, Shaun applies himself to the phone again. He gathers Esther is pleased.

SHAUN'S DIARY

Thursday 12th January

While Esther is looking at Ben's film from yesterday, I start to telephone the medical team at Cambridge. First is Professor Roy Calne. Normally on *That's Life* when you try and talk to any distinguished figure, you find that he or she is away in Japan, or on a lecture tour in South America, or recovering in hospital from an appalling bout of malaria. But as luck has it, Professor Calne is in Cambridge. I explain to his secretary, Audrey Campbell, that we know about Ben – that we desperately want to help, if we can. She puts me straight through to Calne himself.

I ask him why there is a terrible shortage of donors for child organ transplants. He reiterates the reasons he has already given Debbie. Doctors and paediatricians are too afraid or upset to ask the parents of a child who has just died, parents who are obviously very distressed, whether the organs of their child may be used. The doctors too get very distressed – they don't like losing patients; they feel a terrible sense of loss and failure, sometimes almost guilt. So the questions don't get asked, and as a result there are hardly any suitable organs available for transplants in children.

It seems understandable in one way. Perhaps it is impossible to approach parents who have been bereaved in this terribly tragic way. But then, as Professor Calne reminds me, these doctors and paediatricians are professional people, with a job to carry out. Unless they broach the subject, however hard it may be to do so, Ben and all the other children like him who need liver and kidney transplants will die. If they could only ask, then perhaps instead of two children dying, one might live, and as those bereaved parents began to get over their immediate grief – although nothing, of course, could ever bring their child back – they would know they had given another child at least the chance to live.

I then ask him specifically about Ben. How desperately does he need the transplant? Professor Calne tells me that it is now a matter

21

of weeks only. Then it will be too late to operate. Ben could live for several more months, but what 'living' will mean then is open to speculation. Already, day by day, his general state of health is deteriorating. But if a liver were to become available today, not only would Professor Calne be willing to carry out the transplant, he'd operate immediately.

But what are Ben's chances? Without the transplant, perhaps no chance at all. He will certainly die. But if he has the operation, he will at least have a fifty-fifty chance – perhaps greater – of getting through the first year. And if he survives that he could well grow up to live a normal life. In America they've started to get very encouraging results – one girl who had the operation when she was five is now just starting university, fifteen years later.

I ask him if Ben should be sent to America, if the chances there are so much better? Professor Calne repeats that he has the surgical skills, the hospital can cope with the occasional paediatric organ transplant. The problem in Britain is that there simply aren't any donors. If the situation continues as it is at present, Ben will die because of the shortage of donors. In America, where children's livers are available from time to time, he'd have some sort of chance. Throughout our conversation, I'm making notes; catching his phrases in a kind of long-hand smudge only I can read. I thank him, and explain that we'll be using his comments on the programme on Sunday. His idea, that organ donation might actually be a comfort to the bereaved parents, is crucial to the story. It is such a persuasive argument. 'I'd be grateful if you would not mention me by name in the programme,' he says. That's a considerable blow. I decide to delay the decision until I've spoken to Esther and Gordon. 'I'll pass that on to my bosses,' I tell him.

I put the phone down, but the thought process goes on in my mind. Here is this brilliant surgeon, with all the skill to save children's lives, denied the means to do so. How do they manage to get the donors for operations on children in the States?

Among the sheaf of letters Debbie gave me is one from the parents of Todd McNeely, the little boy she'd read about in *Reader's Digest*. It's lunchtime in England, breakfast time in New York. There's just a chance the McNeelys will still be at home. They aren't. I try another number on the letter. It turns out to be the Children's Liver Foundation, a trust set up for children suffering from liver disease. They give me a New York number. At last. Stephen McNeely comes to the phone. He's mystified at first. He's never heard of *That's Life,* and since it was his wife who wrote to Debbie and knows the story, he's never heard of Ben Hardwick either. But after a short time I convince him that this really is the BBC in London calling, and explain why we need to know his son's story so urgently. He begins to tell it. It started so tragically, like Ben's – but ends, unlike Ben's, so happily.

The diagnosis that Todd had biliary atresia was made soon after he was born. When he was a year old, the doctors had told his parents to take him home and let him die peacefully. There was no hope. 'Take him home, and forget about it,' they said. But the McNeelys couldn't forget – 'How can you forget that your only little boy is going to die in a few months' time?'

They began to research for themselves the whole area of liver disease and discovered that a Professor Tom Starzl, a surgeon in Pittsburgh, was currently carrying out liver transplants. Perhaps he might be able to give Todd a liver transplant? They went to see him. Todd was accepted as a potential recipient, and he was placed on a waiting list – but at the bottom.

He stayed on the list for several months, receiving regular check-ups. It was during their stay in Pittsburgh for one of those routine examinations that Stephen and Linda were suddenly given the chance of a transplant for Todd. Although he was still low down on the list, a liver that was his blood group had become available in a nearby hospital. Livers have to be used within six hours of removal from a donor. Did the McNeelys want to give Todd this chance?

It took Stephen and Linda no time at all to reach their decision. Todd had the transplant. 'Three years later,' Stephen tells me, 'he is just like any other five-year-old. Rushing round the house and garden like a bull in a china shop. We have to give him one drug every day which ensures that Todd doesn't reject the liver. That's a small price to pay. Without the operation, Todd would have died three years ago. Thanks to those brave parents who agreed to let their child become a donor, Todd has been given a chance to live.'

I arrange for a picture of Todd to be flown over from New York. Stephen describes it to me. It shows Todd running through a garden, sun shining on his blond hair – the picture of life.

Next call is to Dr Alec Mowatt, Ben's physician at King's College Hospital in London. He is very helpful. He corroborates everything Debbie has told me yesterday, and carefully explains Ben's disease to me. He says nearly a thousand children are born every year with some kind of liver disease. Not all these children die. They don't all require transplants – only a handful need this ultimate form of treatment. In most cases of liver disease, the earlier the diagnosis, the better the chance of treatment and cure. In Ben's case, no, there is no hope. No hope of treatment effecting a cure, no real hope of a transplant.

I go over the story in my mind. All the pieces of the jigsaw are assembled. I tell Esther I think I now have all the information we need to write the script. 'Do you mind if we go back to my house to write it?' she says. 'I want to go home now, and be with my children.' I remember that Joshua, her little boy, is almost exactly the same age as Ben Hardwick.

We drive back together to her home in Kew. As she opens the front door, like a breath of fresh air we find three wildly dancing children, fighting excitedly for our attention. They scream life, health and hope at us – every child's right. But not every child's destiny. Esther lifts them in her arms. Then she heads towards the desk in her study.

CHAPTER THREE

The script of *That's Life* is designed to sound easy. The viewers are led through the details. If the story isn't clear the first time they hear it, it never will be clear. There is no second time. Sometimes a script is wrestled out of months of research, files and documents. Esther's floor has often been carpeted with company searches and copies of contracts that she and the researcher have to pick their way through. Sometimes it is only at this scripting session that a particular awkward question occurs to her for the first time – and a hole appears in the story that sinks it, so that it has to be abandoned.

Ben's story is different. Debbie has done so much research for us – Shaun's efforts over the last day and a half have filled the gaps. Both Esther and Shaun are riding on their emotions, their feeling of urgency. 'If only we do this right,' she says to him. She doesn't dare admit her real hope – that somewhere in the audience on Sunday there might be someone who could actually save his life – a doctor who could overcome his own anxiety and, with the picture of Ben in his mind, mention life-saving organ donation to bereaved parents in his care. It seems an absurd hope, and yet . . . in the history of *That's Life* so often help has been forthcoming, viewers are so incredibly sympathetic and caring.

Shaun and Esther sit together in the study, Shaun with a glass of white wine, Esther pounding the typewriter. Her team keep all drink away from her until she has finished a script, otherwise her already erratic typing becomes the clumsy dance of a hippo playing chopsticks. Esther wanders into the next room, where Joshua is playing with Desmond. Clearly the identification between her own baby son and Ben is painfully close. But equally clearly she must not let that personal feeling overbalance into the script. 'This story is writing itself,' she tells Shaun. The letters from Calne, the film of Debbie and Ben, the story of Todd, all link together.

Then, a snag. Esther types Professor Calne's name. Shaun intervenes. 'He doesn't want us to name him,' he says. Esther stares at him. 'But we must,' she says. 'Suppose donors do come forward, they must have a name to contact. Why doesn't he want us to name him?' 'I reckon it's a professional thing,' Shaun says. 'Maybe he thinks it will arouse jealousy, or he'll be accused of publicity-seeking.' 'Can you ring him back', Esther asks, 'and explain that it really will make a difference? See what he says, try and persuade him.' Instinctively she believes that if they just describe Calne anonymously, someone, somewhere, may just forget which hospital. That vital offer could go astray. Shaun makes a note to ring Calne tomorrow.

SHAUN'S DIARY

Friday 13th January

'We've been scooped,' Gordon greets me as I walk into the office. On his desk he has a copy of yesterday's *Daily Express*. On the front page is a photograph of a little girl called Gemma Knight. The headline runs: MOUNTAIN OF HOPE FOR BABY GEMMA. The large photograph shows Gemma sitting amidst a pile of the thousands of letters that have been sent to the Knight family since her story was featured in last Saturday's paper.

Gordon has ordered up a copy of the original story. Under the headline FOR THE LOVE OF GEMMA – HEARTBREAK PARENTS PLEAD FOR £250,000 TO GIVE THEIR BABY A LIVER TRANSPLANT it tells how Gemma will die within a year if she doesn't have a liver transplant; it says her only hope is to go to America for the operation. The story seems just like Ben's. Gemma had the kasai operation when she was just a few months old and it hadn't worked. Then the Knights learnt of Professor Starzl in America. They had been in touch with the surgical team in Pittsburgh and Gemma was given a number of preliminary tests before being accepted as a possible transplant patient. But her parents had been told that they would have to put cash up front. The *Express* is publicising the family's plight in the hope that its readers will raise the money needed.

Gordon is worried that we will be carrying the same story. But, of course, we aren't. Esther quickly points out that our story,

26

although it is about a child with the same liver disease, is not about sending him to America. The transplant operation could be performed in this country. She shows Gordon the script she's written last night. 'There's no doubt that the idea of being able to take Ben to America is one immediate solution,' she says, 'but it isn't the real answer. It needn't be the answer for Gemma Knight either. These operations should be done here. The skill is here; they want to perform them here. If that little girl does go to America she'll have to join a waiting list of other children. She could die waiting to get to the top of the list. Even if a liver becomes available they'll have to offer it to an American child before they can offer it to Gemma. Can you imagine the outcry there'd be over there if Gemma were seen to take the place of an American baby? Going to America has to be a lottery of sorts. And anyway this operation should be carried out here.'

We decide to add Gemma's story to the script. Now, looking through the item, Gordon feels we've got the right balance. We have to be very careful to avoid the suggestion that Gemma should not go to America, but at the same time to point out that Ben should not *have* to go there for the operation.

CHAPTER FOUR

Sunday, studio day. Like a witch's brew, all the ingredients of the programme are assembled. The performers, the pictures, the camera and sound men, make-up and costumes, eye of toad and leg of frog. Bob Marsland, the studio director, mixes the whole lot, shoves it on the stove, and it's served to millions of viewers at 9.25 precisely.

In theory, it's an impossible programme. It's far too complicated to put together in one studio day, with four hundred different camera shots, a huge collection of photographs and cuttings, and no possibility of editing because it is broadcast ten minutes after the recording is finished. Add to that the unpredictability of a live studio audience, who may howl with laughter at the most unexpected moments, and it's quite obviously insane to attempt it.

And yet, thanks to the skills of directors like Bob, and the tremendous craft of all the technical team, it seems to work. At least, we've never fallen off the screen yet.

At 10.30 in the morning the reporters get into their seats; Bill Buckley, Gavin Campbell and Michael Groth. They've all been involved in researching different items in the office during the week, in between film locations, and they know the background of the Ben story, as it's been developing over the last two days. We all work through the show and after Ben's item, Esther turns to the other reporters. There is a real rapport between them all, a genuine liking and respect. 'What do you think?' she asks. They nod at her. It works, they think. She turns to Joanna Monro, who with Doc Cox is in charge of the jokes that punctuate the show, the misprints and the naughty pictures. Jo looks back, and doesn't say anything. A large tear falls down her face. Well, it may not work on the air, but at least everyone here in the studio is deeply moved. Again that secret hope stirs at the back of Esther's mind. Can we save him?

28

At 7.30 the audience arrives. They settle into their seats, ready to be amused. The programme begins with street interviews, and a policeman is shown threatening to arrest Esther for obstruction again (she already has one conviction obtained while she was offering the crowds bat soup). The holiday camp film gets roars of laughter. And then comes Ben's story. Esther introduces it:

ESTHER: Now usually, as you know, we ask you to write to us rather than ring us up if you have a story because obviously it's much easier for us to understand a story if you do write down all the facts for us. But on Wednesday this week we had a phone call in our office from Debbie Hardwick who lives in Chessington in Surrey. Her story is quite simple, but desperately urgent. She said:

BILL BUCKLEY: 'My little boy, Ben, is two years old. He's going to die in the next few weeks. We need help. You are our last resort.'

ESTHER: We asked: 'What's wrong with Ben?' She said:

BILL: 'He has a liver disease – he was born with it. It's called biliary atresia. And although the doctors have tried to save him with two operations, they couldn't. They said he would die when he was two – he's just had his second birthday.'

ESTHER: 'Can anything save his life?'

BILL: 'Yes, a liver transplant – it can be done.'

ESTHER: Until she said that, we hadn't realised that you could transplant a liver. We said so. Debbie said:

BILL: 'No. People don't know about it – even doctors often don't know it's possible for a child; it's a new operation. But I read in the *Reader's Digest* about the case of the little boy in America who was saved by the operation and I was so desperate for something to save Ben that I rang America. I spoke to the mother of the little boy there who had the liver transplant three years ago. It saved him. He had the same disease as Ben. He was the same age as Ben when he had the transplant. The surgeons said if they'd had to wait just a few more weeks, he wouldn't have been well enough to have the operation. And they're saying that about Ben now. She told me a professor in Cambridge has done successful liver transplants on adults and he's just starting to perform operations on children.'

ESTHER: So we spoke to the professor in England, Professor Calne at the Addenbrooke's Hospital in Cambridge. He told us:

MICHAEL GROTH: 'The problem is that it's virtually impossible to obtain livers for children in this country.'

ESTHER: Which is why Ben is almost certain to die. The professor said:

MICHAEL: 'The liver of an adult is too big for a child. For a baby like Ben it would have to be from a child of less than seven or eight. And if a suitable child does die, as you can imagine, doctors and paediatricians are too afraid or upset to ask the parents who're obviously very distressed, whether the liver of their child can be removed. It's very harrowing for the doctors, too. And they're afraid of making the request at such a tragic time.'

ESTHER: So it looks as if Ben is going to die because no one can actually bear to ask another parent to make the operation possible. We asked the professor whether a transplant would have a good chance of saving Ben. He said:

MICHAEL: 'He'd have at least a fifty-fifty chance. In America they started these operations twenty years ago. One little girl had the operation when she was four – she's fifteen now. Without the transplant she wouldn't be alive today. I want to give Ben that chance, too.'

ESTHER: Then we spoke to the father of the little boy Debbie had read about – Todd McNeely – who lives in New York. Mr McNeely told us:

GAVIN CAMPBELL: 'When Todd was one, the doctor told us he would die. They said he was so ill that there was no hope for him and that frankly we should take him home and just forget it. But can you forget it knowing that your only child is going to die? We thought about it all the time. Eventually we discovered that a liver transplant could save his life. We went to see the surgeon; he gave us hope for the first time. Todd was put on a waiting list and they managed to do it just in time. That was three years ago.'

ESTHER: 'How is he now?'

GAVIN: 'He's just like any other five-year-old. Rushing around like a bull in a china shop. We still have to give him drugs so that his body doesn't reject the liver. But that's a small price to pay. Thanks to the parents who agreed to donate the liver of their child, Todd has been able to live.'

ESTHER: Well, because parents of children who die in America do allow the liver to be donated, children like Todd are saved there. And that's why the *Daily Express* this week has been raising money to send Gemma Knight to America for the operation. But it could be done here if the livers were available here.

Twenty-five babies in this country are born every year with this disease who would be suitable for this kind of operation. At the moment, they all die without it. When Debbie discovered that the operation had saved children like Ben in America, she wrote to Professor Calne in England asking if he could operate on Ben. He wrote back saying, no. Because, he said in his letter:

MICHAEL: 'In fact it is virtually impossible to obtain livers of the right size in the United Kingdom to transplant into children. I think it really is up to public opinion and the paediatricians to come to terms with providing donors for children in the same way that donors are found for adults with liver disease.'

ESTHER: That's why Debbie rang us. That's why we went to meet her and Ben. Though it is difficult to believe, as you watch him, that this gorgeous little boy has only a few months to live at most. Debbie told us how she felt when she first got the professor's letter saying there are no livers available for children like Ben in this country and that the operation to save his life is just not possible. She said:

(*Film*)

DEBBIE: I was heartbroken . . . just heartbroken. Suddenly they said there's just no chance for Ben, he will die. Every day you wonder if it's going to be your last day especially if you tell him off for anything, and you put him to bed and you think 'Oh God, is he going to get up in the morning?' You just don't know, he could actually die tomorrow. The only chance for him is a transplant and there's just no livers available.

SHAUN: How urgently does Ben need this transplant?

DEBBIE: He needs it quite urgently, because he's already living on borrowed time. I mean, we nearly lost him just before Christmas when he was in hospital with septicaemia and the hospital told us that he would die. He went into a liver coma and he was very very ill. But he's so strong that suddenly he was better . . . he was just over it and he was home again. He's such a happy child, you never hear him cry as such, so on occasions when he's not very well and he cries, it's very frightening, because you think 'Is it now, am I going to lose him?'

(*Film ends*)

ESTHER: We checked this with Professor Calne. He told us:

MICHAEL: 'During the next month or so, Ben's health will continue to get worse. If it gets much worse, it won't be possible to do the operation – we need to do it as soon as possible. If we could find a donor I could do the operation tomorrow.'

ESTHER: The professor believes that the operation could, in the long run, almost be a source of hope for bereaved parents. He told us:

MICHAEL: 'If the doctors could only ask the parents, then instead of two children dying, one might live. And although nothing can bring their own child back, at least they'll know there's another child that they've given the chance to live.'

ESTHER: In this case it could be Ben. We asked Debbie if she had a message for any parent who might, tragically, be in a position to save him. That would be the parent of a child of less than seven or eight, who dies. Debbie knows what that tragedy feels like – she lives with the fear day by day. Every evening she spends with him may be their last. As she played with him in the bath, she said:

(*Film*)

DEBBIE: Surely, though, if a child has died, if that child has given life to another child isn't that some sort of consolation to the parents eventually – maybe not immediately – but eventually? Surely it must be some consolation that they have saved another child.

(BEN *calls to* DEBBIE *– 'Mum, Mum, Mum.' Film ends*)

ESTHER: If anyone can help, all they have to do is to tell their doctor. He can make all the necessary arrangements either through a medical organisation called UK Transplant, or with Professor Calne's unit at Addenbrooke's Hospital in Cambridge. And we will, of course, tell you what happens.

All the pieces have slotted together. Professor Calne has agreed to let us use his name. During the film of Ben in the bath we can feel the audience loving him, willing him to live. As the second film ends on Ben's final, imploring 'Mum, Mum, Mum', Esther has to dig her own finger nails hard into the palms of her hands to carry on without a tremor. The programme is over.

In the hospitality room afterwards, Esther is allowed a glass of wine. She, Shaun and Gordon look at each other. Did they do it right? All that evening, and that night, Esther replays the item in her mind. Could we have done it better? Yes, of course, we could. But did we do it well enough? Well, Heaven knows, we tried.

SHAUN'S DIARY

Monday 16th January

9.00 am Officially our day off, the one chance to lie in. A call from the office. Duty Office, which is manned to take calls from viewers about programmes, has been swamped with calls about Ben. Gordon had warned them there might be a great deal of response, and had taken them carefully through the script so they know what to say if, by some chance, a donor comes forward. No donor has come forward.

But every other kind of help has been offered. Spiritual healers have rung, parents of other ill children have rung, other adult liver transplant patients have rung, asking if there is any way they can help the Hardwicks.

And there have been offers of money. Some of them, huge offers. Together they might be enough to fly Ben to America. Hence the call from the office. Will I please start checking these offers out? We must not raise false hopes for Debbie, but, at the same time, we must not risk missing a chance for Ben.

No way have we appealed for money – it didn't even occur to us that this might be a possibility. We'd concentrated on this country, trying to change attitudes here. But suddenly I realise the story may be changing direction. So I begin by phoning back everybody who has offered financial help, to try and establish a realistic total of what's been promised. By 11 o'clock, thanks to the help of one anonymous donation of £50,000, we have nearly £100,000. Of course, these are only telephone offers, and we must very carefully check them out before we release this information publicly. Indeed, another offer of £50,000 turns out to be a rather pathetic hoax. The caller makes four different arrangements to come and see us with his cheque, and each time never turns up. But he is the exception.

11.00 am The office calls me to say that a new offer of money has been received from a man who wishes to remain anonymous. He'll only talk to me and he's left the number of a London hotel. I try the number and speak to his wife. He's had to go out on business but has left a message to say that whatever the cost might be of sending Ben to America, he will meet it.

I call Esther to tell her about the offers. She's ecstatic, but slightly cautious – she's only too well aware that we can only count on the money once it's in the bank. We agree, however, that I should begin to explore the medical side of Ben's being given the operation in America.

I start with the Children's Liver Foundation in the States, who helped me find Todd McNeely's father. They help again, this time giving me a number for Professor Starzl in Pittsburgh, the pioneer surgeon specialising in liver transplants for children. The woman I speak to at the Foundation is fascinated when she hears about our programme, and the story of Ben. She says history is repeating itself. It is because a child was dying in the States, and President Reagan himself had appealed on TV for donors to come forward, that the transplant programme for children has really gathered pace. She tells me that there is an official at the White House, the 'agency liaison officer', Michael Batten, who acted as co-ordinator for the President's appeal. Mr Batten, she says, is still concerned, because the President is himself still interested in the continuing success of the transplant programme.

In the middle of talking to the Foundation, we are suddenly interrupted by the operator. She says there is an urgent call for me, a question of life and death. The operator connects our producer Bryher Scudamore, who tells me that someone from a Northern Ireland police station has rung to say that they think they might have a suitable liver from a young child. I can't believe it. Here is the offer we need – but why have the police wasted precious time by phoning our office rather than getting straight through to the hospital? I immediately call the police station and speak to an inspector. He apologises and says that it is too late; before the first call had even been made to the office it seems that the liver had been cut open in the mortuary.

I am devastated. To have been so close. I ask the inspector why he phoned us rather than the centralised transplant service, UK Transplant? He says he's never heard of it. This response seems quite alarming. If police stations don't know about such important co-ordinating centres, who *can* be expected to know?

As soon as I put the phone down, it rings again. Gavin Campbell, one of the *That's Life* presenters, has just taken a call from a lady in North London; he feels that I should hear the message she left:

35

Our son Thomas died last April. He was just three months old. We weren't asked whether we would donate any of his organs. If we had been I'm sure we would have said yes. We would have been delighted to give another child the chance to live. There was nothing we could do for Thomas, but knowing he had helped another to live would have made the grief much easier to bear . . . the thought of giving life to someone else. At the time there is so much else going on in your mind that you don't think about things like that. But I'm certain that the idea of being asked would not be difficult to accept. Thomas has a twin sister. If she were to die now, we would willingly offer her liver or anything if it could help save another child. I think no mother or father would refuse this.

This mother most eloquently proves Professor Calne's point to us. Bereaved parents can be comforted by the idea of saving another life.

I begin to realise how much impact Ben's story is making already. Early in the afternoon the *Standard*, London's evening newspaper, calls to ask for permission to speak to the Hardwicks; a local radio station wants to do a phone-interview with Debbie. I phone Debbie to ask if she wants to speak to them and she tells me that her own phone hasn't stopped ringing all morning – either enquiries from local newspapers or friends responding to the programme. She says that suddenly she is filled with hope for the first time in the year since the doctors told her that Ben would die. I tell her that we've been offered quite a lot of money; she asks how much. I don't want to raise her hopes, so I say that it's impossible to tell, but that if the offers continue to come in as they have done this morning, it might be worth examining the possibility of sending Ben to America.

After speaking to Debbie, I think I should try to reach Professor Starzl in Pittsburgh again, but, once more, I fail. Thinking over the possibility of sending Ben to America, I decide to ring Peter Hardy, the *Express* journalist who wrote the stories about Gemma Knight.

I congratulate him on the success of his story and ask him how much is now in the trust for Gemma. '£150,000 or thereabouts,' he replies, 'and we'll need at least that to pay for the operation and everything else.' He then analyses the costs for me. If the operation goes smoothly, with no complications, it will cost about 53,000 dollars. Any complications and the cost could instantly rise to as much as 250,000 dollars – the post-operative care in particular will be very expensive. Allowing for the additional cost of finding a house for the parents for the six to twelve months that they are likely to have to stay in Pittsburgh, first of all waiting for a donor to come up and then for the six or so months after the operation, he has arrived at his final bill of about £150,000. The flights between England and America will all be free, as many are needed; they will be a gift from British Airways, for whom Stephen Knight, Gemma's father, works.

The generosity of British Airways has already been matched for Ben by British Caledonian. They have offered to pay for any flights which he and his family may need to go to America.

It is all beginning to feel much more of a reality, if Debbie wants to undertake the trip. Worried by being unable to reach Starzl, the only surgeon we know of who can perform the operation in America, I decide to take the plunge and call Michael Batten, the agency liaison officer at the White House. He handles personal pleas for help addressed to the President. The Children's Liver Foundation in America have told me how much he helped them. Perhaps now he can help me get hold of Starzl.

Batten is unbelievably helpful. He says that he will get a message from the White House to Starzl's team in Pittsburgh, and that he will do anything he can to give Ben the chance to live. He reminds me that Reagan appeared on television himself to make a personal appeal for a child needing a liver transplant, and it crosses my mind to wonder whether Mrs Thatcher might do the same. Batten asks me to call him the moment he can give any further assistance.

No sooner have I put my phone down, than it rings again. The man who called this morning, offering to pay for Ben to go to America, whatever the cost, wants to meet me. Can I go to his hotel at 9 o'clock tonight? He feels that we shouldn't waste any time in making the necessary arrangements. I agree to meet him for dinner at his hotel. I had arranged to eat with Esther and Desmond this evening, so I cancel that and leave a message warning them to expect me very late after my meeting with this man.

9.00 pm. He meets me promptly at the hotel lobby, as arranged. Over dinner with his wife, we talk at length about the programme and television generally. He explains that he and his family had just come back from holiday; the first thing they saw on their return yesterday was *That's Life.* They were all moved by Debbie's appeal and want to help in whatever way they can. He is already involved with a number of charities and medical research work, so he sees this offer as an extension of that work.

It's just after midnight and we've worked out a way of financing Ben's operation in America. He has agreed to underwrite the cost of the operation whatever it might be. If Ben needs to, and can, go tomorrow, he wants us to call in all the other money we have been promised and he will make up whatever shortfall there might be from the total cost of the operation. I have explained that the figure of £150,000 is only an estimate, it could be more. He says that he will meet the costs whatever they are.

Driving to Esther's just after midnight, I reflect on this kind of incredible benevolence. There is no reason why this man should be offering so much financial aid; he is already spending hundreds of thousands of pounds every year on other charitable projects. He is doing it, because, like hundreds of viewers who have been phoning in all day with their promises of money, be it a pound note from a child's money box or five pounds from a pensioner's savings, it was what he can afford. Like them, he is prepared to give anything he can to give Ben the chance to live.

I arrive at Esther's just before 1 o'clock. She's fallen asleep waiting for me to get there. I stay about ten minutes, gloomily ringing the doorbell, and then drive back to North London.

CHAPTER FIVE

At the Tuesday production meeting, Shaun brings the rest of the team up to date with yesterday's response to the programme. Not just the phone calls – now letters have started to come in. One from a family in Devon:

> We have experienced the same feelings as Ben's family – our little boy Richard died in 1977 of biliary atresia, just four days before his second birthday.
> When it was discovered that Richard was suffering from the disorder we were told that it was incurable and that he wouldn't reach the age of five. We were grief-stricken, and felt sure that someone could cure him. We were prepared to take him anywhere, even sell the house to raise money, but were told that to take him around to different places would only shorten his life, and could not be successful. It was terrible. We often wonder if our son could have had a successful liver transplant, so to Ben's mother we send our heartfelt sympathy, and hope that something can be done for him.

In 1977, when Richard died, the new wonder drug, cyclosporin, had not yet been discovered. The only drugs used then to counteract rejection (when a patient's body fights to destroy the new organ) were steroids. Steroids have unacceptable side-effects on children, if they are used in high dosages over long periods. So liver transplants were not being performed on children in Britain at the time Richard died.

But since the discovery of cyclosporin, the whole picture has changed. So how is it that parents like the Hardwicks are still not being referred to Professor Calne by the doctors who specialise in treating liver disease? Debbie learned about him by chance, leafing through a back copy of the *Reader's Digest*, and then being referred back to Calne in Britain when she wrote desperately to America. And yet Ben was being treated at the best possible place, at King's College Hospital. Why did they not guide Debbie towards Professor Calne? Either the doctors are concealing from their patients the fact that transplant surgery is performed at Addenbrooke's, or communication between different doctors and hospitals is almost non-existent. Either way the situation seems to us to be appalling, tragic.

We never find the answer to this riddle. Our assistant producer, Bryher Scudamore, receives an anonymous phone call from a man who claims to be a doctor, working in a hospital, treating children with liver disease. He starts to attack the work of the transplant team in Cambridge – he claims they overestimate their own success rate, that transplants on children simply do not work. We never pay very much attention to anonymous phone calls, but Bryher is struck by the fact that this man appears to have a genuine medical background, in spite of his wild accusations.

Esther has had a letter from a paediatrician working in a large hospital in the north of England. He is ferociously angry. How could we mislead our viewers into believing liver transplants have any chance of success, he asks. We are irresponsible in the extreme. Furthermore, he intends to report the doctors we have quoted on the programme to the General Medical Council, for advertising. Esther writes a reply that scorches the paper – then chucks it in the bin and writes another more reasoned response. But she wonders at the savagery of the paediatrician's rage. It seems to spring from a real loathing of transplant surgery – and yet Professor Calne, father of six children of his own, is clearly fighting to save ill children from suffering an early death.

Luckily this kind of antagonism from a few members of the medical profession is more than outweighed by the marvellous letters from other doctors, who say they believe we have made a real contribution to saving lives by reminding viewers about organ donation. Then there are the letters arriving with every post from other bereaved parents. Shaun reads one aloud at the Tuesday production meeting which convinces the team that somehow it must be included in next Sunday's programme. It comes from parents in Northern Ireland. And it more than answers the fears, aroused by that *Panorama* 'brain death' programme, that organs may be removed too quickly. In fact the problem is the reverse, that due to the Department of Health code of practice relating to transplants, and the doctors' overwhelming desire to save their patients, it may be left too late. The parents' letter says, most movingly, that we need not be afraid of transplant doctors, nor imagine them as body-snatchers. Rather, they are caring and cautious, perhaps even too cautious!

Dear That's Life

It's tragic when a young life could be saved but it seems as though nothing can be done. I and my husband know what it's like to watch a child dying. Our son Peter fell off his bike and hit his head and died four days later. We asked the doctors to see if his kidneys would help another child live. They were wonderful at the Royal Belfast Hospital for Sick Children, and although they knew he was dying from the start and also of our offer, at no stage was there any thought on their part of switching off to get at the spare parts, in fact quite the opposite. They were trying so hard to save Peter that in the end his kidneys were of no use as he suffered kidney damage due, I understand, to his very severe brain injury.

What I am getting at is this, please, parents don't believe the tales you hear of doctors just using patients as and when convenient for the parts offered. It's just not true. Their real aim is to save the owner of the prospective parts. (I feel this has been badly put but I hope you understand what I'm getting at.)

Doctors are also slightly to blame – we had no idea that livers were needed and we would have gladly offered Peter's if it had been suitable. If this had been pointed out we'd have been so pleased to help another child.

Peter was seven when he died in September. It upset me so much to hear your appeal for Ben. I just wish I could have helped four months ago, I know it would have helped us too in a strange way.

So please, parents, be brave, and doctors be brave, and ask.

During the production meeting, one of the secretaries brings in a copy of the London *Standard*. With a headline – TIME IS RUNNING

OUT FOR BEN – the paper has taken up the campaign to help get Ben the liver transplant he so desperately needs. There is a gorgeous picture by Stuart Nicol of Ben, once again playing with bubbles in the bath.

The first hour of the production meeting is devoted to the Ben story, the letters, the reactions, the developments. It becomes clear that if Ben is to be sent to America, Shaun is going to have to spend the whole week sorting out the problems and making all the necessary arrangements. So he leaves the meeting at this point, and the team concentrates on the rest of this week's programme.

SHAUN'S DIARY

Wednesday 18th January

A frustrating afternoon, spent trying to find ways of using the money to fly Ben to America. If we aren't very careful, we could find ourselves facing horrendous tax problems. It has happened in the past, to appeals like the Penlee Life Boat Disaster Fund. The trouble is there is no department of the BBC to cope with this kind of problem. I decide to call Ben's anonymous benefactor, and he gets his lawyer to discuss the problem with the Charity Commissioners.

I ring Michael Batten, our contact in the White House, and bring him up to date. To my delight, he tells me that he has now contacted Starzl, and has made preliminary requests for the operation. There are problems, not least because a number of American children are also on the waiting list for transplants. But Ben should be acceptable for their liver transplant programme. He'd have to join the list and come to Pittsburgh with his parents and, as Batten put it, 'stay loose'. It could be months of waiting, he tells me, but if that's what his parents want, if they are prepared to take the risk, then no more time should be wasted. They should apply now. In order to clear a number of bureaucratic problems and to help avoid criticism of Ben seeming to queue jump (even though he wouldn't actually jump but have to wait his turn) Batten wants Ben's parents to make a personal plea to President Reagan at the White House, asking for his help.

In the evening, Billy and Debbie Hardwick send a telegram to the President:

PRESIDENT REAGAN, THE WHITE HOUSE, WASHINGTON DC 20500 USA

DEAR MR PRESIDENT. WE HAVE LEARNED OF YOUR INTEREST IN CHILDREN NEEDING LIVER TRANSPLANTS. OUR TWO YEAR OLD LITTLE BABY BOY BEN HARDWICK DESPERATELY NEEDS A LIVER TRANSPLANT TO SAVE HIS LIFE. WE FEEL BEN WOULD HAVE A GREATER CHANCE OF THE GIFT OF LIFE IF THE OPERATION COULD BE PERFORMED IN AMERICA. PLEASE HELP US TO GIVE BEN THIS CHANCE TO LIVE.

Thursday 19th January

More letters. One couple from Stoke-on-Trent write to say how closely they can identify with the Hardwicks:

. . . we felt very sorry for the family – we know what they must be going through as we lost our child last summer.

As it was, there was no way in which she could be saved, despite all the efforts of the hospital staff, as she had sustained total brain damage. When we were told that the life support machine had to be turned off, we decided that if this was the case then we wished that the kidneys and any other organs should be used for transplant. We were later told that the kidneys had been used to save two lives, and this gave us a little comfort, knowing that our child's death had not been a complete waste but had resulted in saving the lives of two other people. I think this is what made us decide to let our child's death help others to live. We obviously wish we had known about Ben, as something might have been done to help him.

Losing a child is very heartbreaking and the loss will be with us all our lives. A person can never be replaced. But we hope that this letter may help others to decide if their loved one's death will be used to help another person to live.

It is so tragic to read this letter, then turn to this next one, telling of a child who died because no organs were available:

Our son Adrian died in September 1983 at the age of three years and nine months from biliary atresia. We had been in contact with Professor Calne at Cambridge. He replied that he was willing to perform a transplant but our own consultant would have to find the donor. This we knew would be a mammoth task as the public are not aware of the need. We also knew the greatest decision a parent would have to make would be to donate the liver from a child they love.

Sadly we never began a search for a donor as Adrian died the day after we received Professor Calne's reply. We are hoping and praying that through your programme a donor may be found for Ben and others like him.

The more of these incredibly moving letters from such very brave families that Esther and I read, the angrier we become. Why are doctors and paediatricians hiding behind the excuse that bereaved parents should not be asked whether they want their child to become a donor? The people that are writing us by the score are telling us very plainly that it *is* a comfort, that they wanted to be asked, that their only consoling thought amidst such awful despair was the thought that their child had not died in vain, that this death wasn't wholly meaningless. We feel great sympathy for these parents, admire their outstanding courage, and we are left with a residual feeling of anger towards the doctors who can't bear to ask the questions which could save the lives of other children waiting for transplants, children like Ben, or like Adrian, who had died waiting for a donor no one thought could be found.

Clearly, Ben's medical condition can change from day to day. I speak to his physician at King's College Hospital, Dr Mowatt, this morning. Ben is going to be admitted on Friday morning for a series of tests to ensure that his portal vein – a major blood vessel from the liver – is fully open. If it is closed, there will be very little chance of Ben's transplant operation – taking place even if a donor becomes available. It's another obstacle in the path. To us, it's completely unexpected. I ask the physician why no one has told us this before, why don't they know if his portal vein is open; had we made an appeal on air without knowing the full medical condition? He tells me that it is only one of a number of tests. Ben's medical condition generally supports the idea that he is suitable for a transplant; but he would have to undergo this major test before any final decision could be taken.

While he is on the line to me, one of the secretaries in the office tells me that Ben's benefactor is waiting to speak to me. I take his call and explain the present position.

It seems that an individual cannot be the object of a charitable purpose. This man is as shocked as I am to learn that, under our charity tax laws, it is almost certain that using publicly donated money to send Ben Hardwick to America will not be considered by the tax authorities as a 'charitable purpose' even if it's the only chance to save his life. Such a Fund would probably be subject to large amounts of tax.

The afternoon is spent talking to lawyers, accountants, the charity commissioners and advisers to major charities in the UK. By 5 o'clock we all seem to be hitting a brick wall and only getting more and more bruised. The major financial donor calls again. He suggests that he bring together one of the top accountants in the country, his solicitor and several of his financial and public relations advisers, and that Gordon and I meet them all in his city offices at 6.30 tonight.

The meeting has been lengthy, but at last we resolve to set up a research foundation with a trust. The money will be available through this trust and can be paid out at any time, in any country, in any currency as we require.

Free from the stranglehold of red tape, Gordon and I go for a drink together in Aldwych. I phone home to see if there are any messages. Debbie and Billy have called to say that the White House has been in touch. Michael Batten has confirmed that the President's office will make all the necessary arrangements for their visas and permits in the States; that they will arrange accommodation for them; and that they are free to come to the States as soon as they are ready. The White House would await their call.

Friday 20th January

Yesterday was uneventful – there seemed to be nothing I could do except ring and thank Michael Batten for all his help, and promise I would make sure Ben's medical notes would be sent over to the

States with him. Today Ben is due to have his tests in hospital – it is just a scan, and the results will be given almost immediately to Debbie. She says she will ring us as soon as she hears.

The day's post lands on my desk. One letter is from a mother whose son had died, and she had agreed to allow him to be used as a donor. By coincidence, Professor Calne carried out the transplants. She writes:

> I have never regretted this for one moment. I urge doctors at this very painful time, and parents in a similar situation to ours, to donate these vital organs. I draw very great comfort from knowing that my son's life was not a complete waste, and that because of him, other children live.

I read on. More letters of sympathy. Then a small batch of letters from animal lovers, accusing Professor Calne of using animals to test his new techniques. True, he does, but only to save human life. Sadly there is no other way to test a new surgical method, or the effects of a drug like cyclosporin. They mention cyclosporin in their propaganda leaflet – they claim it is a drug that cannot be used to save human life. How wrong they are. If they have a case, why do they ruin it with these false claims, I wonder. The next letter I come across puts all their hysteria out of my mind. It comes from a mother in Hull.

> My daughter had a little girl born with biliary atresia. My daughter found it difficult to cope, and so I looked after the baby. Her name was Louise. Just after she was born she had an operation to try and cure her liver disease. It didn't work. They said she had two years to live.
>
> I wrote to the professor and the doctor in London. He invited me to take Louise to see him if our specialist would give permission. I was told by her specialist it would be a waste of a journey as nothing could be done.
>
> Then I read in the *Star* that President Reagan had granted permission for a sixteen-year-old girl to have a liver transplant in America. By this time I was about frantic trying to get someone for Louise. I asked Louise's doctor if he would write and try to get a transplant for Louise on our next visit to him. He

had found out though that for Louise to have a transplant it would cost three quarters of a million dollars. Where can anyone get this kind of money? The baby had only a few months to live – there wasn't time. We then came to realise that we could do no more and hoped and prayed for a miracle which never came.

Louise started to deteriorate and eventually the sad day came. While sitting on my knee she died. She was cremated and her ashes are still in a casket on my sitting-room window sill.

The purpose of this letter is to tell Ben's mum not to build her hopes too high but to give her child twenty-four hours a day love and affection. This letter would never end if I wrote everything I could about this awful illness.

It is a long morning, waiting for Debbie to ring. By lunchtime we start calling the hospital to try and find her – Ben's had the test but she's left the hospital. I ring Dr Mowatt. He says that he's not yet heard the results of the tests but he'd try and find out what's happened and call me back.

By the middle of the afternoon we've still heard nothing. I phone Debbie at home – she's just got in. Ben's tests had been inconclusive. They couldn't tell what condition the blood vessel – the portal vein – near his liver is in. If it is blocked, the operation will be impossible. If it is open, then the transplant is on and he can leave for America immediately. But this result is neither one thing nor the other. I try to reassure her that at least this means there is still hope.

While we are talking, a call from Dr Mowatt comes in, on the other line. He wants to talk to me about the results of the latest test. They plan to take Ben into hospital again on Sunday. This time they will have to give him a general anaesthetic, and then a test called a angiogram. Blue dye will be injected into his blood stream, so that any blockages or leakages in his blood system will show up on the scanner.

I tell Esther – she starts to pace around the office. 'Why put a child through an extra general anaesthetic?' she demands. 'He's delicate enough, are all these tests really necessary? Surely Professor Starzl can do them in America, if he believes they really must be done?' I admit it all makes me feel a bit nervous on Ben's behalf, but there seems to be no alternative. Ben is booked in for the Sunday, and we set about arranging flowers and toys to be taken to him while he's there.

I'd better check with Michael Batten to see if Professor Starzl needs these tests done over here. As it happens, he was just about to call me. He has been in touch with Starzl, who is prepared to do the operation, although Ben will have to join a waiting list. The visas, and all the other administrative problems have all been resolved, through the White House. When can Ben and his parents come? I can't believe it. Suddenly it is all fixed. I tell him I'll talk through everything with the Hardwicks, and call him back later that evening.

I try Debbie's number. She is out. I ring Addenbrooke's Hospital, and speak to their transplant co-ordinator, Celia Wight. Is there any news? Yes, this week they have been offered five livers, but none suitable for Ben. While I'm on the phone to her, Esther passes a letter to me. It's from one of our viewers, who has received a liver transplant. She writes praising Professor Calne and his team in Addenbrooke's. She owes them her life. I read it all to Celia. She says she has seen many letters like it. I can't help feeling, in spite of all the money that has come in, in spite of all the help we've had from the White House, it will be such a pity if this operation has to take place in the States.

I take the letter down to the script room, and Esther and I sort through the material for this week's programme.

We go over the past week's events, the wave of support from viewers determined that Ben should have the chance to live, the involvement of the White House in the case; and we conclude with the statement Debbie has asked us to read:

Billy and I can't believe how generous *That's Life* viewers have been. We never thought that people could care as much. For the first time since last April we now have real hope, thanks to you. We never dreamt this might even be possible. You've given Ben the first real chance to live that he's ever had. If going to America is the best chance for him to live, then we will just have to go tomorrow.

Ben with Debbie and Billy, on Shaun's first visit

Below Turning the tables on the photographer

Todd McNeely – three years after the operation, he is like any other 5-year-old

Below An apprehensive Ben and Debbie on arrival at Addenbrooke's

Right Struggling to stay awake . . . but the effects of the premed at last overwhelm him

Overleaf Ben in intensive care

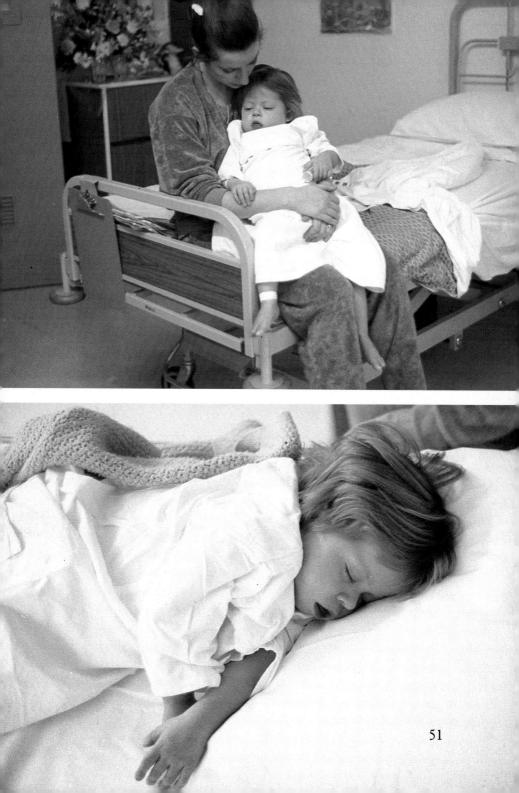

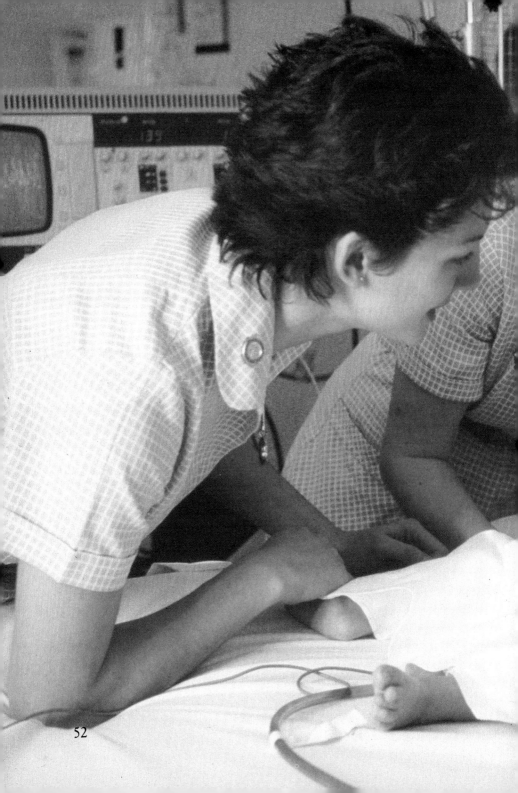

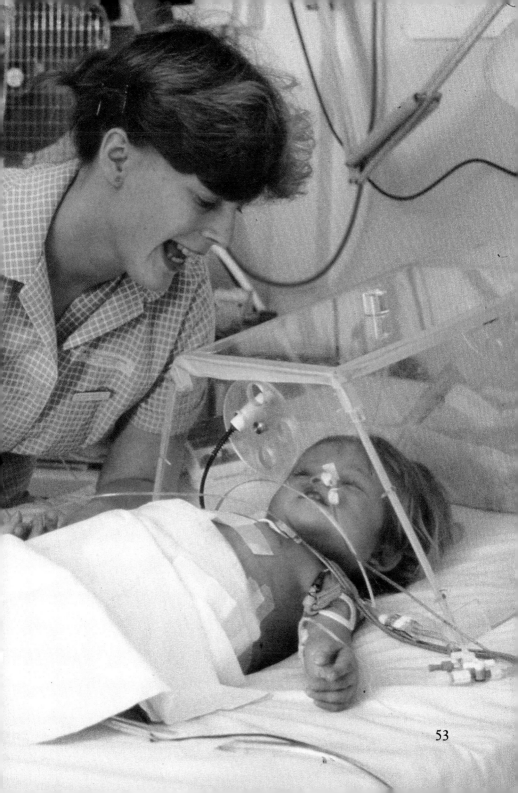

53

The meeting between the
two families.

Inset The picture
of Matthew that
Julie Fewkes gave
to Debbie

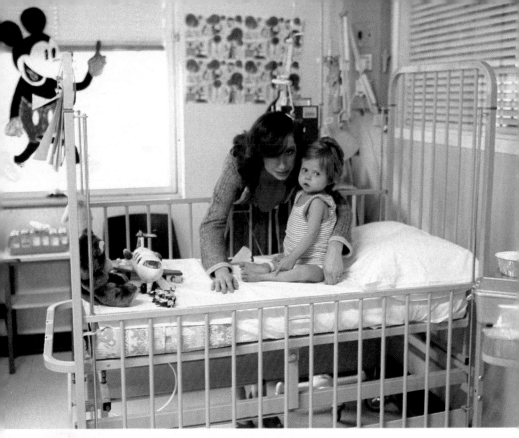

Back in his own room at last.
Ben is still very frightened
at this stage.

Left His grandmother, Joyce,
comforts him

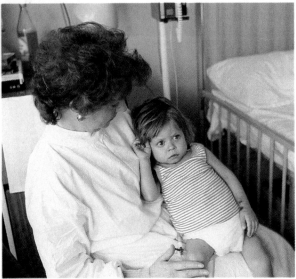

Right With his favourite
teddy

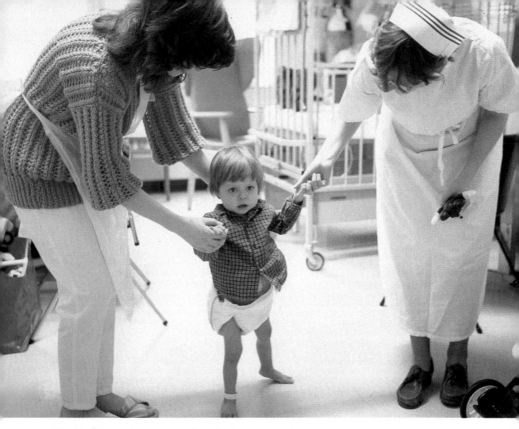

Ben takes his first uncertain steps after the operation

Left and right A game with a bowl of bubbles and a tube of smarties mark further stages in his recovery

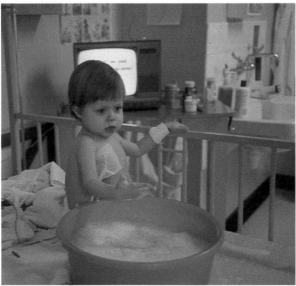

58

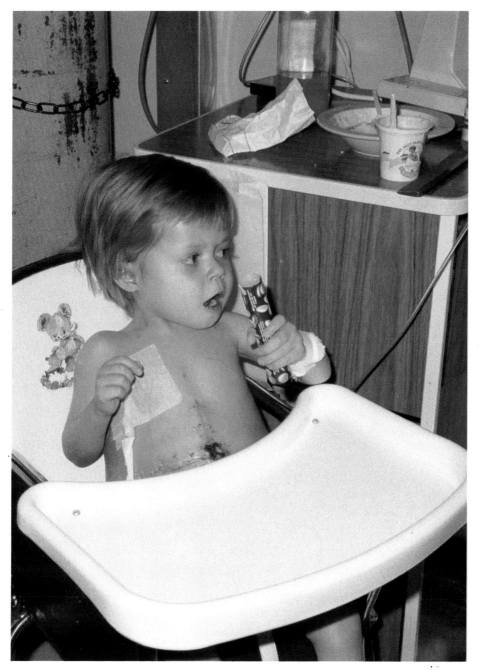

A trip to the hospital shop is an important first outing

Right Racing up the hospital corridors

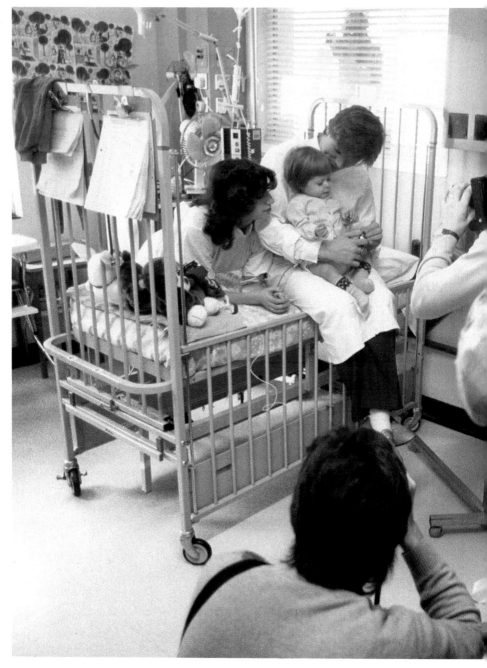

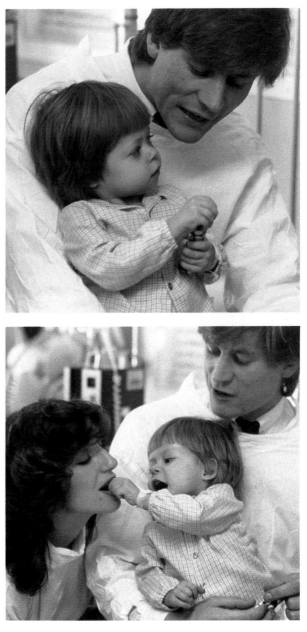

Ben, Debbie and Billy face the press photographers

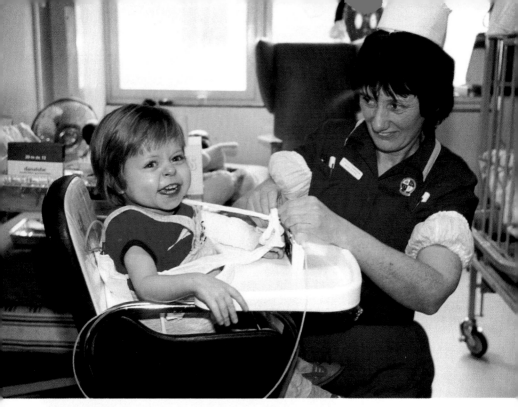

Sharing a joke with Sister Townrow

Left Esther meets Ben at last

At about 7 o'clock we are back in the main office, just about to leave, when my personal phone rings. It is Debbie.

'What do I do?' she begins. 'The hospital in Cambridge has just rung me and said can I bring Ben straightaway to Cambridge. They think that there's a liver which will be suitable. They want him tomorrow and they'll do the operation straightaway. What do I do, Shaun?'

I'm completely lost for words. As Debbie continues speaking, I scribble down on a slip of paper what she had just told me and push it over to Esther. I ask Debbie what she thinks she should do; what's her gut reaction? She doesn't know. What about her husband, Billy? He doesn't know either. Once again she asks me what she should do. I say we're not the people to tell her, not in our role as programme makers, anyway. If we do give her advice, it will have to be as people who have become her friends.

Esther by now is sitting next to me, aware of the conversation. 'Do you think I should talk to Debbie?' she asks. I nod. I hand her the phone. Esther listens to Debbie intently. Then she says, 'Do you want my advice, not as a journalist, but as a friend?' Debbie says, 'Yes. You know the facts, what would you do?' It's a heavy responsibility. For a moment, Esther wonders how she will feel if things go wrong. But having read all the letters, knowing the skill of the team at Addenbrooke's, knowing how other British children will depend on this decision, she plunges ahead. 'I can only say that if Ben were my son I would take him to Addenbrooke's. If he goes to America, he has to withstand that long journey, and then maybe wait for weeks, or months. Ben could die out there before a suitable liver is donated. Now you know there is one waiting for him, here, I would take this chance, if Ben were mine.' Debbie sighs. 'That's how I feel,' she says. 'But Billy doesn't agree. I think he dreads it so much, now the moment has arrived. He hates to think of Ben on that table.' 'Would you like me to speak to him?' Esther asks. 'Yes,' Debbie answers.

It's a terrible moment to talk to Billy for the first time, but now Esther has started, there's no going back. 'What would you do then?' Billy asks. Esther goes over all the arguments on both sides. There is no doubt Professor Starzl has many years' experience, and a marvellous success rate. But if one liver were donated, and Ben was waiting for it, but so was an equally desperately ill American baby, the American must take priority. There was no guarantee an operation would come in time for Ben. At least there is the offer now.

There is silence at the other end of the phone. Then Billy says, 'That's it then. We'll have to go to Cambridge.' From his voice, Esther realises he believes he has just sentenced the baby son he adores to death. Debbie takes the phone back. They talk for a minute or two longer. Esther says we will all be thinking about her, and Ben. They say goodbye, and slowly Esther puts the phone down. She sits, staring into space. Clearly she is terribly worried that she may have been wrong to have given such unambiguous advice. But who else can Debbie turn to? We have done so much research, talked to the experts in the States, talked to Cambridge. We have no particular axe to grind, all we want is the best, for Debbie and for Ben. Let's hope none of us will ever regret it.

Desmond, Esther's husband, takes us both out to a local bistro for dinner. He is extremely sympathetic, as always, and does his best to take our minds off Ben. But of course all his efforts are in vain. Nothing could possibly stop us thinking about Ben.

We leave the restaurant, and go back to phone Debbie at home. How are things? She tells us tonight she has found it impossible to put Ben to bed. Tonight, more than any other night. 'He's being so lovely. I want to be with him all night, just playing with him. I can't think about tomorrow, not now.'

Saturday 21st January

Esther and I spend most of the morning trying desperately to think about anything other than Ben, but find it impossible. Debbie phones mid-morning to say that she and Ben have now arrived at Addenbrooke's Hospital; Ben will spend the rest of the day going through various minor tests. No news of the operation. Certainly it isn't going to happen today – most likely tomorrow morning.

Sunday 22nd January

As soon as I wake up I call the hospital in Cambridge. There is still no news of the operation and Ben has been allowed to have breakfast. Since you are not allowed to eat for at least six hours

66

before general anaesthetic, I assume that the operation won't take place this morning. Opening the curtains I notice the snow on the ground outside – I wonder whether the delay in the operation is a result of the weather.

Shortly after 8 o'clock Esther calls. We arrange to meet Gordon at the television theatre in an hour's time to plan the day ahead and make the script changes for the programme this evening.

Arriving just after 9, the three of us settle down to a programme conference. It is decided that I should go up to Cambridge and liaise with Gordon from the hospital. He very much wants to have a link with the hospital all day so that we can give the latest news in the programme. He suggests we might even transmit a live, down-the-phone interview with Debbie from Addenbrooke's. Armed with flowers, toys for Ben and a wedding anniversary present for Billy and Debbie (Esther had only learnt earlier in the morning that today is their anniversary, and had scoured the house for a suitable gift), I set out for Cambridge.

I haven't seen Ben since the original interview we did. Once again I find myself quite unsure of what to expect. Walking through the children's ward, staring through the glass screens at bed after bed of sick children, listening to the sound of laughter from the playroom, I remember the first time I had been in hospital as a toddler. I had been terrified. It was only an operation to remove my tonsils and my mother was with me, but the whole thing was so traumatic that until a few years ago I found it almost impossible even to go inside a hospital. I think that Ben must probably be terrified, too.

I walk into his room. It is empty. Immediately I think that the operation has begun – we've got there too late. But then Debbie walks in. 'Oh hello, what's wrong?' She's noticed the panic in my face. 'It's okay, Ben's just been taken to the loo by my mum.' Then Ben comes back in, holding the hand of his granny, Joyce Arnold.

Still nothing has been said about the operation. Ben has now been given nearly all the tests he'll need – chest examinations, heart tests, blood tests – he's utterly fed up with being prodded and poked, and shows it every time a doctor comes near him. Whenever he sees a white coat he screams at the top of his voice, 'Mum, Mum.'

I find the transplant co-ordinator, Celia Wight, and we talk about

Ben's forthcoming operation and about the risks involved in someone so young. Then she tells me that she doesn't want any publicity about the operation on the programme that night. Please don't mention it at all, she says.

I tell her that's impossible. I can't believe she means it. We'll have to report the latest news, millions of people will be hanging on, waiting to hear. If we know the truth, how can we conceal it from them? She's terrified of the effect this may have on the family of the child who's likely to be the donor. It seems that the operation may be delayed at least until tomorrow. The parents have been asked, and have given their consent, but of course they may change their minds at any moment. If we even mention on the programme that Ben is in hospital, she's worried that the newspapers will start to hunt for the family of the donor. This will put the hospital, the doctors and nursing staff looking after the donor child under tremendous strain. Such intense pressure might, she cautions me, even mean that the parents of the donor child will refuse to allow their child's liver to be used. 'I'm sorry, I just don't think you should tell people about this. It might ruin everything.'

She begins to talk more generally. Since last week's programme the number of organs the hospital's been offered for all transplants – hearts, lungs, kidneys, corneas, livers – has multiplied dramatically. 'It's all because of your programme. We've battled away for years and years to bring this problem of finding child and adult donors to the attention of doctors and patients. The story of Ben has managed to do more than we have in just one week. There's no doubt that the liver which we hope to use for him has become available as a result of your programme.'

I seize my chance again. 'But don't you think that if that really is the case, if we have helped your work so much in just one week, that we can go on helping? People trust us. You can trust us. Obviously we don't want to do anything at all which could jeopardise the chance of Ben getting his transplant, but I'm sure that we could work out a way of keeping people informed. We owe it to all the thousands of viewers who have shown they care, by offering so much help.'

Celia is still unsure so I call Gordon Watts in London and he talks to her. She is becoming more convinced that we won't put Ben's operation at risk but her reluctance continues. Gordon puts Esther on the line who guarantees that everything we say on the programme will be agreed beforehand with Celia and Professor Calne. Celia consents.

Late afternoon, and we have finalised our statement. We will tell viewers that Ben is waiting in Addenbrooke's Hospital in the hope that a transplant may become possible in the next few days. This will be followed by a phone call between Esther and Debbie. It is an odd compromise. We are still not allowed to say that he is being prepared for the operation now – we can only say that it is possible. Let's hope the truth gets through to our audience.

For Ben it has been a very long day. Tests most of the morning and afternoon. Just a short break for lunch – chicken, one of his favourite foods. Throughout the day Ben has clung feverishly to Debbie or to Joyce, his grandmother. Sometimes he'll be cheeky and call Debbie, 'Deb', then chuckle.

Just after tea Debbie is asked to go upstairs and have a look at the intensive care ward and the room where Ben will be taken immediately after his operation. She leaves Ben with me. Watching him, playing with him for these few moments, I feel that each second is a year, each matters so much.

Since the operation is almost certain to take place the following day, I decide that this is likely to be the last evening for some time that Debbie will be able to get away from the hospital. I think that it would be nice for her to go out for dinner so I call Richard Ballantine, a friend of mine who is a doctor, and ask him to join us after the programme. It will give Debbie a chance to talk to someone who actually understands some of the medical and technical things that had been discussed with her during the day, but which she has been unable to take in.

Debbie puts Ben to bed, leaving Joyce to sit with him, while she and I go off to make the phone-link to the programme in London. Just as she had in her earlier interview with me, Debbie remains perfectly calm while we wait for Esther to come on the line. We can hear the audience laughing as they watch the film which precedes the Ben story in the programme. Then we hear Esther mention Ben's name. She tells the week's story and brings the viewers bang up to date:

ESTHER: The news we have for you now is about Ben Hardwick, the 2-year-old little boy who has the terrible liver disease, biliary atresia, and isn't expected to live very much longer. We've had some marvellous letters this week, letters from parents who've lost their own children and who say they only wish a doctor had asked them permission to donate their baby's liver to save another child's life. May I just read one of those letters? The parents have asked us not to give their names. They say:

'We lost our little boy through a cot death three weeks ago. No words can describe how we feel, and at the time of his death it was hard to take in what anyone was saying, but if only we had been asked if we would mind them taking his liver or any other organ, I think it would help some of the pain we're feeling now.'

And they end by saying 'I carry a donor card. Could a card or something like it be made for a child? Surely something can be done to save all these little lives.' We've had a number of letters like this one, and people have been sending money.

BILL: Marc Chandler, who lives in Rainham, wrote to us, 'I'm sending you my £1 pocket money for baby Ben to help send him to America for the operation.' And, as you can see, he attached a cheque.

He wasn't alone. So many people have sent us money that we've had to open a special bank account, which we've called the Ben Hardwick Transplant Appeal Fund, and in one week we've been promised £150,000. Which means, as Marc Chandler says, that Ben could now go to America for a transplant operation.

ESTHER: Ben's mother, Debbie, told us this week:

GAVIN: 'We are completely overwhelmed. We just never thought people could care so much. For the first time, we have real hope now. We never dreamed this might even be possible. Your viewers have given Ben a chance he didn't have until this week. If going to America is the best chance for him to live, we'll go tomorrow.'

ESTHER: That's what Debbie told us on Friday. But suddenly, this weekend, everything changed. The transplant co-ordinator at Ben's hospital, Addenbrooke's Hospital in Cambridge, Celia Wight, rang to tell us that it's not just money that's been offered. She said:

GAVIN: 'Immediately after your programme was over, we started getting calls from doctors and hospitals all over the country. We've had a dramatic increase in the number of organs of all kinds we've been offered for transplant this week. Since your programme doctors have had the courage and confidence to ask parents, and parents, remembering your story about Ben, have found that saying "Yes" to doctors' requests is perhaps the only positive moment during the worst time in their lives. People's whole attitude seems to have changed.

'We've battled and battled away to bring the problem of finding child donors to the attention of doctors and parents for three years. The story of Ben managed to do more in just one week.'

ESTHER: And among those offers from brave parents has come one which may mean Ben's life can be saved. He's now at Addenbrooke's Hospital with Debbie because they believe, in the next few days, a transplant may be possible. In fact, she's on the phone now:

(*Picks up phone*)

Hello, Debbie. How are you?

DEBBIE: Not too bad, thank you.

ESTHER: And how's Ben?

DEBBIE: Oh, he's very well. He's sleeping at the moment.

ESTHER: Well, you must be feeling a mixture of hopeful and fearful.

DEBBIE: Yes, it's hard to describe how we feel, really. As you say, it's a mixture of the two.

71

ESTHER: I wonder if you have anything to say to the people who have been in touch with us, offering transplants and offering money?

DEBBIE: Well, I've got too much that I want to say to them all. Thank you isn't enough to any of those people, especially to anybody who could save our son's life by donating the liver of their child. They can give him the gift of life, which is more than I ever dreamed of, really.

ESTHER: I wonder, Debbie, if I may read one other letter to you, because it's from a lady who very much wanted her thoughts to go to you. She is somebody who, three years ago, had a liver transplant herself at Addenbrooke's Hospital with the professor who is looking after Ben now. And she says:

'I owe my life to Professor Calne. We should all give thanks and praise to God for such a brilliant surgeon in this country. I would like you to pass on this message of hope to Debbie and Ben: just keep praying for strength for Ben until a liver does become available. I know it will.

  'Till then, my thoughts and prayers will be with Ben and his family.'

I think she speaks for us all, Debbie. So we'll be thinking of you, over the next few days. Thank you so much for speaking to us and thank you for the message to our viewers. And, of course, love to Ben.

DEBBIE: Yes. Thank you.

ESTHER: Thank you, Debbie.

(*Puts down phone*)

Well, to all the people who so generously sent money for Ben, we must also say thank you. We've spoken to some of the people, who say they'd like it used to save babies like Ben. We're now going to find the best way to do that.

  In the meantime, as Mrs Stanley says in her letter, 'Our thoughts and prayers will be Ben and his family.' Good night.

After her interview, I take Debbie and her mother out for a meal. The waiters manage to wheel a television into the room, near our table, so Debbie can watch the programme. We listen to Ben's story, in silence. We aren't alone. All the other guests, and the hotel staff, are crowding round us, watching too. Afterwards they come over to Debbie, one by one, to wish her luck.

I'm called away to the phone. It's Esther, wanting to know how Debbie and Ben are. Debbie talks to her for about ten minutes. On another phone Sharon Knight, the mother of the little girl being flown to America for the same operation, has rung the hotel to wish Debbie good luck. In Sharon's voice I can hear trepidation, and doubt. She asks me if Debbie is really sure this is the right thing to do? She can, after all, still change her mind. I decide not to pass those doubts on to Debbie. I tell Sharon that I will pass her love and best wishes on, and I do.

11.45 pm. Debbie and Joyce have gone back to the hospital. I tell Debbie she can ring me whenever she likes, if she needs to talk. I fall asleep almost at once.

2 am. The phone rings suddenly, hideously, in my ear. It's Debbie. For a moment I dread she may have terrible news for me. She explains she just can't sleep. She keeps wondering, over and over again, if she has done the right thing. I hope I give her the right answer. 'You had no real choice,' I tell her. 'This was the chance you've been fighting for. It's the only chance for Ben. If it fails, you know that he only had a few weeks of life left, anyway. But if it succeeds, even if he only lives an extra six months, or a year, you will have given him that extra time. And every extra day with him is precious.'

CHAPTER SIX

The Monday morning after the programme, Esther is early into the office. The previous night's show had been a very odd one. The Ben script had been completely rewritten, of course. Originally it had described the sudden opportunity to take Ben to America. Suddenly we had to change it all, to explain that instead of America, Debbie had rushed him to Addenbrooke's. Then we had to explain why, without properly explaining why. If only we had been able to say that he was being prepared for a transplant operation today.

We needn't have worried. Although we had stood by the agreement with Celia, the message has come through loud and clear from Esther's conversation with Debbie. And now, wandering round the office, unable to concentrate, two families are constantly in her mind. The Hardwicks, with the unbearable suspense of the operation ahead of them. And that other family, the unknown donors, who have made it possible. If only we could thank them somehow.

Already we have to start thinking about next Sunday's programme. Gordon and Esther decide that Les Wilson, the programme's photographer, should join Shaun in Cambridge. Les prides himself as a 'heavy' – but in reality he excels either in comedy pictures or in poetic sequences like this one. He knows the Hardwicks from the evening he spent at home with them, photographing Ben. The little boy has taken to Les. Esther briefs him to make a picture diary of the week, and he sets off for Addenbrooke's.

SHAUN'S DIARY

Monday 23rd January. Cambridge

Over to the hospital at seven o'clock. Les Wilson comes up from London so that he can take pictures, both for Debbie, and for the programme, of Ben before his operation.

Ben was awake at seven o'clock this morning. He wanted a drink and some breakfast but the nurses say that he can't have anything. The operation is due to happen at midday.

Debbie feels distressed that she can't give Ben anything to drink or eat; he keeps saying 'Mum, Mum, drink, drink,' but she has to say no. Debbie tells me that she's feeling frightened this morning; she finds it hard to look at Ben without imagining that this is the last time that she will see him alive. She's very scared. 'Can I really do this to him? He seems so well and happy this morning. Can I put him on that table and let them operate? How I wish it wasn't going to happen.'

11 o'clock. No news yet. Snow lies thick on the ground. A reporter from the *Standard* arrives. He is prevented from getting into Ben's room by the nurses. The nurses call for the hospital administrator, Mr Jefford. First the reporter is asked to go and see him and then I am summoned. He tells me that he doesn't want me in the hospital and that I should leave. I explain to him that I am here to give moral support to Mrs Hardwick and this morning am present at her request. He says that if it was up to him I wouldn't be even allowed on hospital premises, but that if this is the wish of the patient's mother, then he has no choice. I may stay, not as a reporter but as a friend.

I go back to Debbie and explain to her what Mr Jefford has told me. Les, meanwhile, has been taking dozens of photographs of Ben. I'm aware that by taking them we risk being thrown out of the hospital since Mr Jefford has specifically asked us not to be here as journalists. But I can only think that if Ben dies, then Debbie and Billy will have a precious record of their little boy this morning. These photographs are for them.

Midday. Still nothing has happened. Ben is crying, very hungry, and desperate for a drink. Debbie feels terrible because she can do nothing to answer his needs. She feels he thinks she is deliberately being cruel to him. She breaks down in tears.

Suddenly the room is buzzing with nurses and doctors. Earlier in the morning we had been told that the medical staff would come to prepare him about forty-five minutes before the operation. So Debbie knows what is going to happen. She moves over to Ben, who is playing with a record player on the floor, and picks him up. 'Come on darling, come to Mummy.'

Ben looks around and sees a nurse moving towards him with a tiny white gown in her hands. He is petrified and screams out 'Mum, Mum, no; Mum, no.' Debbie knows what she has to do but the pain of carrying out the tasks expected of her bears heavily on her and shows clearly in the tortured expression of her face. Lifting Ben from the floor, she carries him over to her bed and starts to undress him. We are all in tears. It's as if Ben knows what is happening – as if he knows that this might be the last few waking moments in his life.

Debbie slips the little white coat over his arms. He struggles frantically. He clearly hates what's going on and is now crying, screaming with unhappiness. How on earth Debbie can actually handle this is completely beyond me.

Another nurse comes in to give him his premed. Debbie sits Ben on her lap, and stroking his forehead, talks gently to him, trying to soothe him. The nurse lifts the spoon with the anaesthetic syrup towards his mouth. Instinctively he turns away. Joyce has to come over and turn his head towards the nurse, prising his lips apart, before he'll take the anaesthetic. He resists the whole way, like an animal refusing its medicine. He tries to spit it out, but eventually he relaxes and swallows it – the only thing he's had to drink all morning. 'Nice drink Ben, nice drink,' says Debbie to him, painfully.

He immediately starts to yell again. It's as if he knows that he's being drugged. The agony of listening to him crying, yelling, then whimpering. Debbie holds him tightly in her arms. He starts to wriggle more and more furiously, resisting sleep with all his mind and body. Debbie turns to me. 'He knows what we're doing. I feel so cruel. I wish he knew that I was only doing it for him, to save him.'

Les is now standing with his back to the room, looking out of the window. I go over to him, and it's obvious that he has been disturbed by what's happening to Ben. The tears are rushing down his face.

By now Ben is almost asleep in Debbie's arms. Occasionally he stirs and tries to resist sleep, but now he has very little energy. I can hear Debbie whispering into his ear, 'I'm sorry, my sweet, please understand, please don't be cross with Mummy.'

She carries Ben, asleep, over to his cot and places him on the mattress. Les takes a picture of him, peaceful now, like a little angel. Turning to Les and me Debbie says, 'I don't want to stay now. I'd like to go. Professor Calne says that it will be at least six or seven hours from now before anything is known. Can we go into town? Anything but stay here. Not now. Please let's go.'

Les takes Debbie out of the hospital through a back entrance. Reporters from most of the Fleet Street newspapers are crowding the reception area and she clearly can't face them. With Joyce and Debbie, Les and I drive away from the hospital, whilst Ben is being lifted on to the theatre trolley and taken down to the operating theatre.

We drop Debbie and Joyce off in the shopping centre; the two of us go back to my hotel. The afternoon passes very slowly. Debbie and her mother turn up just after 5 o'clock with Billy and Debbie's father, Sid. They've decided to go back to the hospital together. Billy wants me to come too.

Once again at Addenbrooke's. There is no news of the operation. We learn that the bad weather had delayed the arrival of the donor organ and that Ben actually went down to the theatre at 5 o'clock. The operation has hardly begun.

8 o'clock. Still no news.

9 o'clock. The district health authority spokesman, John Edwards, arrives. I'd met him a couple of years before when he'd acted as spokesman for the heart operations carried out at Papworth, a few miles outside Cambridge. He takes Debbie aside and briefly informs her that all is going well.

11 o'clock. In the lobby I recognise a *Daily Star* journalist. Overhearing a conversation between him and John Edwards, I gather that the *Star* is trying to track down the name of the donor's parents. The reporter suggests that the family comes from Nottingham. Edwards refuses to comment and disappears back into the theatre.

Les and I sit with Debbie and her mother in the waiting room of the children's ward. Debbie has brought two bottles of champagne into the room. 'I kept these; I knew I wanted to keep them for Ben. I know it's going to be all right. Why don't we hear something? – then I can open them and we can celebrate.'

11.30 pm. John Edwards walks in. 'Mrs Hardwick, it's okay. The little fellow came out of the theatre at 10.58. He's in intensive care now and the operation has gone very smoothly. You can go up and see him in a few minutes.'

It isn't possible to describe the feeling of jubilation which pervades the waiting room at that moment. Debbie opens her champagne and, with her mum, toasts the life which her little soldier may now have been granted. Les and I quietly share their joy, but it is very much Debbie's moment, Debbie's victory.

She phones her husband, Billy, and then her father. I try to call Esther. She has already heard the news. How? Apparently the *Daily Express* had been given the story of the operation's success fifteen minutes before Debbie herself was told. The paper had already rung Esther – they'd been tipped off a good half-hour before we'd heard anything at all in the hospital. They woke her out of a fitful sleep. 'Congratulations!' said the reporter. 'Thanks, but why?' Esther mumbled. 'On Ben's transplant, it's been a great success,' said the *Daily Express*.

I return to Debbie to find her sitting sadly in the corner of the room. Later she tells me that suddenly she'd found herself unable to think of anything but the family of the child who had donated the liver. Not that Debbie knows who they are, or who the child is, not even if it was a little boy or a girl. But she had become overwhelmed by the thought of what they must be going through. She was all too painfully aware that her celebration was also their extreme tragedy.

I try to console Debbie by telling her that somewhere else someone is talking sympathetically to the family of the donor. I hope that they are being told that although nothing really can comfort them in the few hours after their child's death, slowly, gradually, they may derive something from the knowledge that their child hasn't died in vain. Rather than two babies dying, one has been given the chance to live. Perhaps not surprisingly, this is of little comfort to her.

Debbie is asked if she'd like to go up and see Ben. She goes up with her mum to the intensive care unit and Les and I return to the hotel. On our way out we overhear the *Star* journalist talking to Edwards again. He's really on the track of the parents of the donor child now and won't stop until he finds out who the family is and has tried to speak to them.

Tuesday 24th January

Every national newspaper carries a piece about Ben. He has become the story of the day. The *Daily Mail* headline runs SMOOTH OP FOR THAT'S LIFE BOY. The *Sun* – LIVER OP BID TO SAVE TV TODDLER, the *Daily Mirror*, THAT'S LIFE BOY IN HOSPITAL DRAMA. The *Star* gives considerable space to the story – front and inside pages – THAT'S LIFE BOY HAS LIVER SWOP OPERATION, and quotes Esther's comment on the donor family made last night: 'They are going through their own private tragedy. I cannot express in words how I feel about their courage. They have done the most marvellous thing.' Even *The Times* and the *Guardian* carry stories on their front pages.

As I go down to breakfast I'm aware that a number of journalists have arrived at the hotel looking for me or for any lead that will get them to Debbie. They have been banned from the hospital because Debbie has said that, apart from *That's Life*, at the moment she wishes to see no reporters.

Arriving at the hospital I go to see Debbie. Ben is asleep in the intensive care unit. She has spent much of the night with Ben, sitting next to his cot, squeezing his hand. His temperature is high, nearly 40° centigrade. She'd at first been frightened of going to see him last night. Finally pushing her fears aside, she'd ventured in to the intensive care unit. His tiny body looked almost lost as it lay motionless on a vast white bed. A body connected to seemingly hundreds of tubes and machines. But she wasn't scared at all when she saw him; not the least frightened. He was just asleep. Peaceful. And alive.

This morning he seems very much the same. Debbie tells me that he did wake early this morning, and opened his eyes for the first time since the operation. But very quickly he lapsed back into sleep. Professor Calne has indicated that surgically the operation went almost perfectly, and I pass this news on to the office. Esther and Gordon want pictures as soon as I can get them. As I'm talking, Mr Jefford, the hospital administrator, appears. Tapping me not lightly on the shoulder, he asks to see me in his office.

The walk to his office suite is spent in silence. We get there and he orders coffee. Once again he tells me that, if he had his way, I would not be on hospital premises. Because of Debbie's request that I should be allowed to stay he has no choice in the matter. But he wants me to know how unwelcome a presence I am.

I stem his cricitism by asking him to share in my joy over Ben's operation. He must be very pleased – it's a great distinction for his hospital. Almost grudgingly he acknowledges his satisfaction. It does seem odd, even with all the demands that are being made on him at this time, that in these hours of triumph all he can spare me is anger.

Our discussion continues. Has he considered the impact of Ben's operation – not least on the family of the donor child and family – I ask, but he is convinced there is nothing to worry about. The family is quite safe and well protected from the media. 'They need protecting,' I suggest. 'In the next few hours the journalists of at least one Fleet Street newspaper will be on their doorstep, asking for their story.'

Mr Jefford is clearly very worried about the pressure he is now facing from the journalists who are crowding the lobby of the hospital. Ben is the biggest story of the week, and everyone wants a picture of him and Debbie. Everyone wants a story. His desire to have me off the premises is obviously sparked by this: once I'm away, then he can have all journalists removed from the hospital premises with ease. As it is, all the reporters know that I'm in the hospital, with access to Debbie and news about Ben. Whenever they are asked to leave they retort that it's unfair that a BBC journalist is allowed to stay on the premises. From their point of view, perhaps it is. But I know Debbie is relying on me. She has asked me to stay. I can provide sympathy and information if she needs it – she knows I will leave her alone whenever she wants. She knows that I've been asked by Gordon to stay as long as she needs me.

Shortly after lunch Debbie shows signs of not being able to take any more pressure. She is continually besieged by requests to make a statement or appear for a photocall. I advise her to make a brief appearance for the cameras. Since she has just come from Ben's bedside she can give them any little piece of information about his recovery that she can remember. Bravely marching out, escorted by the area administrator John Edwards, Debbie confronts the press. Amidst a battery of flash guns and microphones she tells them, 'He looks well. He opened his eyes and stuck his tongue out, which is one of his friendly little gestures.' Adding to this the official statement from the hospital that Ben is 'stable and satisfactory', Edwards brings Debbie back inside and she returns to see Ben.

I meet Professor Calne for the first time this afternoon. I want to talk to him frankly about Ben's chances of recovery, and the future of the transplant programme for children. When you interview some specialists it can be very hard to evoke any kind of animated reply – you have to do a lot of prodding and legwork to get even a three-word answer from them. But Calne gives me everything I want, and more.

He begins by assuring me that the operation really has gone very well indeed. He has been concerned that the kasai operation Ben had been given as a two-month-old baby might have made surgery complicated. But this had not been the case. The first part of the operation had involved actually unpicking the surgical work from the kasai operation which had bypassed a section of his intestine by joining one part of the stomach to part of the bowel. This stage had gone very smoothly. Next he had had to take out the liver. Looking at it, he had recognised that Ben's liver was in a very bad state indeed – he had very little chance of living more than a few weeks. Then the donor's liver had to be grafted on.

The arrival of this liver had been held up because of the snow. It had been arranged that a plane would bring the liver from the hospital where the child donor had died to Cambridge. But the weather conditions proved too bad for a fixed-wing aircraft, and so at the last minute the liver was brought across country by car. Every second had counted, for the liver is only useful for transplant for a maximum of six hours after removal from the donor, and in the bad weather road traffic was moving very slowly.

But the liver arrived in time, and the surgery went well. Calne is very pleased indeed.

Now Ben is to be barrier nursed – everything he touches must be sterilised and germ-free. A nurse will be next to his bed in intensive care twenty-four hours a day. No one can go and see him except Debbie and Billy, and Debbie's parents. All risks of infection, however small, have to be avoided since the slightest virus or infection at this stage might kill Ben. This intensive care could last for two or three weeks, perhaps more.

Ben will be given special drugs to prevent rejection of his new liver. But these drugs have a side-effect. They will actually lower all his natural body defence mechanisms against infection. Even the common cold virus, which would hardly affect the average child, could possibly take Ben's life, at the moment. It will be some time before he can be normally exposed to the air most of us breathe. Bit by bit they will reduce the doses of the anti-rejection drugs as his own body defence mechanisms re-emerge, to protect him from common bugs and viruses.

Calne is very aware of the effect that the outcome of Ben's operation will have on the future of paediatric and adult transplant surgery. Nevertheless he is relatively confident that things should go well for Ben. Although Ben is the youngest child ever to undergo liver transplant surgery in Britain, just before Christmas, on 13th December, Calne had carried out a liver transplant on a fifteen-year-old Italian girl called Maria. He shows me a photograph taken of her eating turkey on Christmas Day, and he tells me that today he and his colleagues had given her a party to celebrate her leaving the hospital to return home to Italy.

Quickly he moves to the general issues. The shortage of donors is, of course, the biggest problem; Ben may have got his transplant but today literally thousands of people are waiting for kidney, liver, heart, lung, cornea, pancreas and other kinds of transplants. There are at least another ten children he could operate on at once, children for whom a transplant is their only hope. Left much longer, they will be too ill for surgery. And there are still a further sixty or seventy children who will need a transplant in the next couple of years.

The problems of finding the resources actually to carry out this number of operations, even if the donors became available, are considerable. Calne needs a bed in an intensive care unit, specially staffed for this purpose, if any significant transplant programme is to go ahead. But, of course, without the livers there is no possibility of carrying out the surgery at all, and this is his main concern – will the number of offers, which has multiplied several times since we took up the issue, actually continue?

All this is the province of the transplant co-ordinator, Celia Wight. She explains to me that in 1982 there were 3000 patients needing kidney transplants. Only 1000 of these actually received the transplant they needed. The rest were kept alive by dialysis – but as Celia points out, while this may be for many their only hope of staying alive, the almost daily ordeal of going on these machines is not the solution they most want. They want to be able to lead a normal life – the kind of life that most of us expect – and a kidney transplant would give them that life, give them their independence back.

Celia feels that only a complete change of attitude by the public and the medical profession will put right this chronic shortage of organs. People need to realise that these transplants actually save many lives. She explains that although she is employed as a transplant co-ordinator, she can only work inside her own regional health authority. She travels round as many hospitals in East Anglia as possible, talking to the doctors and nursing staff of intensive care units there, explaining to them how vitally these organs are needed and how they can contact her fast if a donor comes forward. But it seems as if there is no national network to inform staff outside her region of the procedures they should take. UK Transplant is supposed to fulfil this role – and some consultants we have spoken to have never heard of UK Transplant. Desperately needed donors may be being lost every day. Shouldn't the Department of Health be taking a stronger lead?

I leave Celia's office and go to see Debbie. She is sitting amidst a huge pile of letters and cards from *That's Life* viewers. She is quite overwhelmed by the response from hundreds of people, many of them children sending home-made cards and offering their own favourite toys to Ben. Debbie says that she wants to thank everyone for their kindness. She would like us to film an interview with herself and Billy tomorrow, which we can show on the programme next Sunday.

CHAPTER SEVEN

On Monday night, at 7 o'clock, the phone rings in the *That's Life* office. We have no means of taking calls after hours – every year we remind ourselves how useful it would be to install an answering machine to record viewers' calls if they desperately need to get in touch with us. Every year we are daunted by the effort required by the technical problems of feeding all our many extensions and direct lines through it. This year we really must do something.

But by great good luck film director Tony Chapman is working late in the office. The call is from the senior information officer at the Trent Area Health Authority. Some of the Fleet Street reporters are hot on the trail of the donor family, and beginning to bay dangerously close to their front door. They are very recently bereaved; it is important that their act of generosity and compassion should not then turn them into a target for press persecution. Trent Authority, who know the parents, believe that their example can be the inspiration for others to follow. To satisfy all the reporters, and to save the family from constant pursuit, they are calling a press conference tomorrow, Wednesday, at 10 o'clock in the morning.

It leaves frighteningly little time for us to find a film team and get there – to the Queen's Medical Centre in Nottingham. Rapidly Tony rings Esther. She calls Gordon. He decides to send Esther and Tony together to Nottingham, while Shaun is interviewing Debbie in Cambridge. Soon after 7 o'clock next morning Esther is on the train trying to plan the interview ahead. The information officer has said that the parents particularly want to speak to *That's Life* . So, after the full press conference, he has arranged for us to meet and talk to Esther in another office. We need only shoot a few feet of film at the press conference, just enough to show it happened, but concentrate our main effort on the interview.

Esther begins to rough out her question-lines on a card – not because she intends to read it, parrot-fashion, to the parents, but because it helps to prepare her mind. But there are so many unknown factors. How did the baby die? Will the parents be able to cope with the memory? Do they know they have given Ben the chance of life? It seems utterly unlikely, with a terribly ill child of their own, that they could possibly have watched the programme two Sundays ago, and seen the lovely little boy to whom they had given this most precious of gifts. Perhaps it was just chance. After ten minutes, Esther has written one question on her card: 'At this moment, is the thought of your baby being a donor, perhaps saving another child's life, painful for you? Or is it, perhaps, a kind of comfort?' That, after all, is the message for other parents, and doctors – and these parents, above all, are the ones who know the truth – whether it is a source of additional pain, as many doctors fear, or of comfort, as Professor Calne believes.

Queen's Medical Centre is a marvellous modern building, set next to the newest medical school in Britain. Tony and his crew have already set up their cameras in the room which is being used for the press conference. Television news crews are there, dozens of radio interviewers, arranging their microphones in the front row. And there are perhaps forty reporters. They are frankly not a pretty sight. Cultivating a kind of professional boredom, swapping casual jokes, they look like a tatty pack of hyenas, even down to the cackles of laughter that rise from them. No wonder the staff at Cambridge so mistrust us. Is this really a picture of journalism in action?

The senior officer comes in the room and calls for attention. Suddenly all the notebooks are out, the cameras ready to roll. 'Ladies and gentlemen, may I explain why we are calling this press conference this morning? As you know, the parents you are about to meet, Mr and Mrs Fewkes, agreed that their own baby son could be used as a donor for organ transplantation. His liver was used for Ben Hardwick. You will also meet the consultant anaesthetist for their son, Mr Jardine, who will be able to answer any medical questions you may have. I would ask you to remember that Mr and Mrs Fewkes are very recently bereaved, I know you will treat them as gently as possible. I would ask you also to use this opportunity to ask any questions you have for them, please do not follow them home. We know that Mr and Mrs Fewkes need privacy, and time together, after experiencing this great tragedy in their lives. We have called this conference so that you may have all the information you need, and in the hope that everyone will now leave Mr and Mrs Fewkes alone. I hope you will respect that. If you are ready, ladies and gentlemen, I will now bring Mr and Mrs Fewkes and Mr Jardine in to meet you.'

Now there is complete silence in the room. A couple walk in, Darryl Fewkes, tall and blond, with an open face. Julie Fewkes, dark-haired, dark-eyed, a little awkward. The bearded man walking behind them is Dr Jardine, the consultant anaesthetist. Television lights flick on, cameras flash into life. What an ordeal this must be for them.

The couple sit down and lean forward, waiting for the first question. There is silence. The hyenas have turned back into humans. No more cackles, no professional boredom. Perhaps it was just a defence, after all. Nobody wants to be the first to ask questions of this couple, who have suffered so much, and risen above it to make such a generous act. A young man clears his throat. 'Mrs Fewkes, when did you first know your son was going to die?' 'We knew from the time he was born. Matthew was disabled from birth.' She speaks softly, but quite calmly. You can feel the room relaxing. This couple are going to cope. Trent Health Authority were right in their assessment. 'How did you feel when you were asked if Matthew could be used as a donor?' Darryl Fewkes answers this time. 'We were glad. It meant our child would be saving another life.' 'Did you know it was Ben?' 'No,' Julie says. 'We would have done it for any child. But we're glad. We can't wait to meet him, if it's possible.' The questions become technical, and Dr Jardine answers them. Then it's over. No tears, no agony. The Fewkes have told their story clearly and with tremendous dignity. The press have responded with compassion and gentleness.

The senior information officer catches Esther's eye and nods towards the door. As they leave, Esther slips out after them. She runs down the corridor – Julie Fewkes turns towards her. Esther opens her mouth to say something – nothing comes out. Instead Esther finds her own face covered with tears. After all this, when the Fewkes have been so controlled, so dignified, she could kill herself for breaking down. But still the tears come – she meets Julie's eyes – Julie reaches out her hand and the two women are holding each other. When she can speak, Esther tries to apologise. 'I'm so sorry, you've been so very brave.' Julie smiles. If there was ever going to be a barrier of shyness between them it had gone now, swept away with Esther's tears. They go together to the office chosen for the interview. The camera and lights are ready. The interview begins:

ESTHER: Did it distress you when they asked if Matthew could be a donor?

JULIE FEWKES: I was pleased the doctor asked us, actually, I was glad they asked us straightaway. It has really helped us a lot to know that Matthew did not die in vain, that he has helped another little boy.

DARRYL FEWKES: We are really glad – not only for Ben. I think we would have done it for any other child anyway. But seeing the programme, my wife and I are just thrilled to bits.

ESTHER: I hope you realise that everybody cares so much about Matthew. We realised what you must be going through and I think everybody really was thinking about you, as much as they were thinking about Ben. Of course Ben is a lovely little boy – does it help you now, knowing what he is like?

JULIE: Well, we have seen him on your programme on Sunday, but we had no idea that the liver was going to go to Ben. As soon as we knew, we were really pleased, and we just pray for him to get better quickly. And we can't wait to see him, and meet his parents.

ESTHER: I think Debbie is a bit nervous that you may feel that there she is, with a little boy who may have survived, and there you are, having lost Matthew. She may feel guilty.

JULIE: There's no need to feel guilty. We're glad Ben is doing all right, we listen to any news we can get of Ben. We are hoping it is all good news and he makes good progress. We know what she is going through, because Matthew has had quite a lot of operations. We knew Matthew was not going to live. If it was the other way round, I would not feel guilty. It is our decision, and we made it.

ESTHER: I think it is also true to say that even if Ben doesn't pull through, of course we are all praying for him, you have achieved an enormous amount. You have made it possible for doctors like Dr Jardine to approach parents now, when they didn't feel they could. I think you are saving lives now that you didn't know about.

JULIE: Yes, it is a wonderful thing.

ESTHER: Have you any message for any other parents who may be going through what you have been through?

JULIE: Well, we just hope that they would think about it, and make a good decision, that they will say, yes. I would have walked all the way, if it was Matthew that wanted a transplant. I would have walked and asked the parents myself. I think most parents would say yes.

ESTHER: We are told Ben would not have lived more than a couple of weeks.

JULIE: We didn't know that. We knew he didn't have long.

ESTHER: We were told it was a matter of weeks. You have given them hope.

JULIE: I know. We just want to meet them and meet little Ben.

ESTHER: Well, Matthew certainly has not died in vain.

DARRYL: We don't think so. And it has released some of the pressures on us if we have given some life to someone else who would have died. It would have been two lives lost, instead of one. We just pray for Ben every night, that he is going to be all right. In our minds we think he will, if his mum and dad love him. We just hope he pulls through. We hope for the best.

ESTHER: Thank you both very much indeed for talking to us.

As they leave the hospital, Esther walks down the corridor with Dr Jardine. They start by talking about the hospital, and he tells her that they perform many kidney transplants there. 'Is that how you knew about Ben?' Esther asks him. 'As a matter of fact, no, I had no idea transplants were possible on children as young as this. But the night of your programme I was ill in bed, with flu. My wife watched the programme by herself, and then came up to me with a cup of tea. She asked me who did these transplants on such young children. I said they must be done at Addenbrooke's but I told her I hadn't heard of them before. She had obviously been very moved by the story of Ben.

'As it happened, the next day I had to act as the anaesthetist for Matthew Fewkes. It was one of a series of operations to try and correct his disability – he had very severe spina bifida. Sadly, it didn't work. By Wednesday, when I came to see him, it was clear to me that he had suffered serious brain damage. So I approached his parents.'

'Was that difficult for you?'

'I've done it before, for kidney transplants. I don't find it difficult because I've never found that parents mind. I know how desperately these organs are needed – and if you explain it may save another life, or put another child out of the agony of constant dialysis, they understand. Certainly the Fewkes didn't hesitate.

'The other problem was the operation to remove the liver, after Matthew had died. It must be kept intact; it took a couple of hours to perform that operation. We handle it very carefully.'

Another nightmare dispelled – that perhaps the donor child is hacked about. In fact they treat the removal of the organs as carefully as any operation. Afterwards the donor child is restored for burial with the greatest care. No parents need worry that their child will be mutilated.

'So if your wife hadn't seen our programme . . . ?'

'It would never have occurred to me that Matthew's liver could be used.'

So Esther's secret hope was justified. The realisation floods her mind. If Debbie hadn't rung us that day, if Mrs Jardine hadn't watched that programme, maybe Ben would be dead now. Or at best, be on his way to America. Liver transplantation would be just another operation possible in America, impossible for British children. She thanks Dr Jardine for all his help, and rushes to phone

Shaun in Cambridge. She tells him everything she's just learned. Then another thought strikes her. 'Julie Fewkes is desperately keen to see Ben. It might be a great comfort to her to be able to talk to Debbie.'

Shaun says he'll tell Debbie. Then he comes back to the phone. 'She doesn't think she can talk to Julie. Now's not the time. Maybe later on, but not today.'

'Give her my love. Is Ben all right?'

'He's fine,' Shaun reassures her. 'Tell the Fewkes Ben is doing fine.'

Esther does so, straightaway, and Julie's huge dark eyes warm with pleasure. 'Just as long as Ben does well,' she says. 'That's all we ask. That's what we're praying for, and we believe he will do well.'

CHAPTER EIGHT

SHAUN'S DIARY

Thursday 26th January. Cambridge

The office rings to say the interview I did with the Hardwicks yesterday looks good. It's the first time they've seen Ben's father Billy. He can't talk nearly as readily as Debbie, but somehow that makes it all the more touching. He clearly had believed he'd killed Ben by agreeing to let the operation take place. Now he can't believe that his son is not only alive, but that he's holding out his arms to them, he clearly knows them, and is asking them to take him home. Not that anyone dares to think about that possibility yet.

Mountains of presents and cards continue to arrive. In the interview Billy picks out a letter from a little boy, Charles, who has sent Ben his favourite toy, a frog. Debbie picks out another letter from a mother whose little girl died of biliary atresia. She explains to me that she wants to show the mother that these children, although they couldn't be saved, have not been forgotten.

Esther tells me the interview with the Fewkes also went well – both films will go into this week's programme. Debbie and I have seen all the reports in the newspapers about the press conference in Nottingham. Headlines like OUR PROUD GIFT OF LIFE TO BEN in the *Daily Mirror*; OUR CHILD DID NOT DIE IN VAIN in the *Daily Express*; and COURAGE OF PARENTS WHO GAVE LIFE TO LITTLE BEN in the *Daily Mail*. Now there is a second name to put beside Ben, Matthew Fewkes.

The office continues to receive sackfuls of letters about Ben's story. Among today's is one from a mother in Northumberland who wants to tell us about her baby son who died when he was just two months old. He had a rare heart condition and had spent all his very short life in hospital. His mother has written to us:

What a blessing it would have been if our little boy had also been a donor and saved another life. To us it would have meant that we hadn't lost him totally and that part of him, however tiny, would have lived on.

Another letter comes from a parent who is now desperately hoping that a child donor may be found for her child. He needs a kidney transplant and time is running out. Already this little boy has had one kidney transplant – his mother had been the donor. Sadly the transplant hadn't worked. The little boy is now on dialysis three days a week. At night he goes to bed with the same prayer, 'Please pray that a kidney will come up for me tonight Mummy.'

Then there is a letter which I find and keep in my diary, just in case. It's from a couple, Irene and Bill Whittaker, who live in Burnley. The tone of the letter is very calm and rational. Their plea is very direct. Perhaps this is why their clear but powerful letter has such an impact on everyone in the office:

> . . . seeing Ben on the television was like seeing our own son Matthew at that age as he too was born with biliary atresia. We were also told by Professor Calne that it was extremely unlikely that Matthew would see his second birthday (we weren't told of liver transplants at that time). Matthew has become however a medical miracle. He celebrated his eleventh birthday last November. No one has been able to explain why he is still alive. He has however suffered a great deal during those eleven years. He has been close to death several times, had two major operations, several minor operations and we have lost count of the numerous blood transfusions. We believe his tremendous will to live has pulled him through.
>
> Unfortunately however Matthew is becoming tired and beginning to lose this will. He wishes to be like other children, wear clothing like other children and not be likened to the 'incredible hulk' because of his colour. His greatest wish is to be able to wear a pair of tight jeans – his enlarged abdomen has made this impossible.
>
> Because of these things we too have written in the past week to Professor Calne to ask him if a liver transplant would be

possible for Matthew. We feel Matthew at least deserves a chance of a normal life. We would be very grateful if our son could be saved. Your programme and efforts have given us hope after all this time. Thank you once again.

Later that evening I go to see Debbie in hospital. Ben has been allowed a little drink – a kind of syrupy mouthwash – although he can't have very much, just a few drops. He is thrilled with it – and can't have enough. In the afternoon the doctors had detected a noise on his chest and he appears to have a few small problems with his breathing. They discuss putting him on the respirator again, but decide it won't be necessary.

Sunday 29th January

Gordon has been very struck by the interview with Mr and Mrs Fewkes. 'I never cease to be amazed,' he tells Esther, 'at the extraordinary way people like Julie and Darryl can express themselves. The sheer goodness they transmit.' He decides the film must finish the programme, together with a reference to Matthew's funeral the next day. But this is to be a story of hope, of courage, of compassion. It begins with the diary of last Monday, day of the operation, illustrated with Les's beautiful still photographs of Ben, and shows the film of my interview with Debbie and Billy. Next comes my discussion with Professor Calne about Ben's operation.

Then Esther turns to the other family, the Fewkes. She tells the story of how Dr Jardine's wife just happened to hear about Ben Hardwick on *That's Life*, and how when Matthew Fewkes tragically died, Dr Jardine approached his parents, Darryl and Julie. We show the moving film of Esther's interview with Darryl and Julie. And then Esther concludes the programme with these words:

They are remarkable people, aren't they? It will be a memorial to Matthew, of course. Indeed, to give life or the chance of life to another person must be one of the best memorials you can have. So our thoughts are with Darryl and Julie Fewkes. Tomorrow morning is Matthew's funeral in Nottingham. Also our thoughts, of course, are with Ben and his family. As Julie said, we'll all keep praying for him during the next crucial week.

93

CHAPTER NINE

On Monday evening, Esther sets off for Cambridge. She has never met Debbie – extraordinary though that seems, when they have seen each other on the screen, talked to each other on the phone so often. Esther is only too aware that although the huge wave of publicity has been a strong weapon in the fight to save Ben's life, it has also taken its toll on Debbie and Billy. She arranges with Debbie to have dinner at a Cambridge restaurant.

They meet like old friends – they have shared so many extremes of emotions over the past three weeks, it could hardly have been otherwise. Over the meal, Debbie starts to tell Shaun and Esther the real cost of the last two years, the immense strain Ben's illness has put on his young parents. Who knows what chance Debbie and Billy might have had together if Ben had been a normal, healthy baby? But living with this gorgeous child, knowing he was, perhaps, destined to die before his second birthday, knocked them off balance. They each responded quite differently. Unable to bear the agony, Billy went out of the house. Sometimes alone, sometimes with friends, anything to distract him from the pain of watching the baby he adores slowly dying in front of him. Debbie, on the other hand, took on the fight with both hands. Outsiders like to believe that tragedy brings people closer together. Often it has the reverse effect. Many couples have discovered, as the Hardwicks have found, that torn by this intolerable strain, they are beginning to drift apart.

'Ben needs us both,' Debbie says. 'We realise that. But I find myself terribly lonely. My mother helps as much as she can.' Esther suggests that maybe some young mothers based in Cambridge might be company for Debbie – nobody seems to know how long Ben will have to stay here, if things go well. But in fact the only people whose company really helps Debbie are the relatives of other transplant patients. They understand, without asking, the swings between hope and despair she will suffer during the months to come.

The conversation moves to the Fewkes family. Debbie is clearly in a huge dilemma. She knows that Julie Fewkes would love to meet her, and see Ben. But the nurses at Addenbrooke's have advised her not to allow it. It will only stir things up, they say. Grief like Julie's sometimes makes people do strange things. Clearly the nurses are worried that Julie may feel Ben is a replacement for Matthew.

Esther says, 'Well, when I met Julie I didn't get the feeling that she would try and possess Ben, take him over in any way. But it must be dreadful for you to know that for your child to live, another child had to die.'

Debbie flinches. 'I just wish it could be different. If only surgeons could manufacture artificial organs. It's dreadful to know that Matthew is dead.'

Esther tries to dispel her feeling of guilt. 'Nothing could have saved Matthew – he would have died anyway. Ben made no difference to Matthew's life, you know that.'

Rationally Debbie knows, but irrationally the death of that other child, one she had never known, weighs very heavily on her. Living closely with the threat to Ben's life for the last two years, she is particularly sensitive to another mother's loss. She can hardly bear to think about the Fewkes' grief. They part: Esther and Shaun to drive back to London, Debbie to return to Ben, in intensive care.

Tuesday. Esther arrives in the *That's Life* office just as the phone rings. It's Billy Hardwick, asking for her. 'Have you seen the newspaper?' She hasn't but while he's hanging on, she does. A large story, claiming the Fewkes are furious with the Hardwicks. The reporter has been to Matthew Fewkes' funeral yesterday, and seems to have constructed the story round the fact that Debbie and Billy haven't sent a wreath. Esther sits numbly, staring at the page. The Fewkes, with their baby son newly buried. The Hardwicks, with their baby son hovering between life and death. What have they done to deserve this? Esther picks up the phone to Billy. 'Try and put this story out of your mind. It's disgusting. Nobody wants to read this kind of garbage.'

'Somebody does,' Billy says. 'We've had a couple of hate calls already – people who've rung without giving their names, just to say how vile we are, not to have sent a wreath.'

'I can only ask you to think about Ben,' Esther says. 'He's worth fighting for. Think about those nurses and doctors, all of them on your side, trying to save your little boy. Tomorrow this stupid story will be wrapping up fish and chips. The day after, it'll be forgotten entirely.'

Shaun comes into the office – he rings Debbie in Cambridge. She too has seen the paper. She is in tears, in Celia Wight's office. Esther rings Julie Fewkes. Julie is equally upset.

'There was a photographer at Matthew's funeral, and I was trying to avoid him,' Julie tells Esther. 'In fact, I had to leave the service too quickly to see who had sent any wreaths. Just as I was coming up the path to our house, I heard the phone ringing. It was someone from the paper. He asked me if I'd seen the wreath from you, Esther, and *That's Life*, and I said no, I was sorry, but I was too upset to see any of them. He read your message on the wreath to me. Then he asked me if I'd seen a wreath from the Hardwicks. I said no. He said there wasn't one. Was I upset? I said of course I was. But I didn't mean I was upset about the wreath – I was upset about Matthew. Wouldn't anyone be, that moment when you come back from your son's funeral?'

Gordon and Esther agree that Shaun must go back to Cambridge. Debbie is alone there, and terribly distressed. To have to cope with this silly scandalmongering, on top of everything else. Esther rings the paper, to try to put the family's point of view to them. The young reporter who wrote the story is adamant: he had spoken to Julie, he says; she was angry and upset. The story was accurate. Esther tries to explain to him the harm this story could do, has already done. She speaks to the reporter's boss. 'Why run something like this? What possible good can it do? Shouldn't you protect these families in their time of tragedy?'

'Mrs Fewkes is a public person, now,' the man says. 'She must expect stories like this.'

'What do you mean, a public person?'

'She's been on television. I've seen her.'

Esther can hardly believe that anyone can have let this story get into print, having seen the Fewkes' compassion and generosity shining from the television screen. 'I know this will come as a surprise,' she says slowly. 'But even people who appear on television have feelings that should be protected.'

Meanwhile there are steps to be taken to try and put the record straight. Billy has had to leave home and move in with friends because the hate calls are still coming in. Julie has been ringing the office, asking if there is any way she can speak directly to Debbie, tell her the truth. Esther says they will see if there is a way to put them in touch.

SHAUN'S DIARY

Tuesday 31st January. Cambridge

The papers are ringing the hospital, trying to reach Debbie. A group of reporters are waiting outside, in case she comes out. I go inside. Debbie is taking refuge still in Celia's office. She is on the edge of tears. I ring Julie Fewkes from the phone on Celia's desk. I want to be able to repeat Julie's words directly to Debbie, so that she can see what a distortion the newspaper report has been. But as I talk, Debbie suddenly grabs the phone from me. 'Julie, it's me,' she says. Within minutes, both women are in tears, tears of relief, and shared emotion.

Debbie hands the phone back to me. Julie asks me if we can arrange for the two families to meet this afternoon. I ask Debbie if this is what she wants – she nods her agreement.

Half an hour later we have arranged for Billy to come up to Cambridge and for the Fewkes to travel down from Nottingham.

Outside the reporters are still waiting to speak to Debbie. She agrees to talk to the London *Standard*. Debbie tries to put the record straight, explaining that her sister-in-law had sent flowers to Matthew's funeral from the Hardwick family. By lunchtime the *Standard* runs a story that begins to repair the damage. TRANSPLANT MOTHER: WE DID GET FLOWERS it starts.

2 o'clock. The Fewkes family arrive at my hotel, Darryl and Julie with their little girl, Victoria. I take them up to my room, and talk to them. Then Debbie and Billy arrive in the hotel lobby. I go down and meet them. I ask them once again if they are certain they want to meet the Fewkes. They are.

I go in first. Debbie and Billy follow me. No need to introduce them of course. In fact, no need for me to say anything. Billy is clutching a large white teddy bear – he walks over to Victoria, hugs her, and gives her the bear. It has been sent by one of our viewers to Ben, but Ben has so many presents, pouring in now by every post. They want Victoria to have it. They sit down together. I leave the room, so that the two families can talk everything over, in private.

I stay away for two hours. When eventually I go back, they are still talking, like old friends, as if they've known each other for years.

I notice that Debbie and Julie are both holding photographs. I ask what they are. They have exchanged pictures of Ben and Matthew. Debbie says how beautiful Matthew looks. She shows me the picture of him, a picture the Fewkes have kept private – refused to give to the press. Matthew was lovely. The photograph shows him smiling, playing on a swing. Julie is just as thrilled with her picture of Ben.

Debbie and Billy have told the Fewkes they will try and arrange with the hospital for Julie and Darryl to visit Ben in intensive care. It's not easy – the hospital does not like donor families meeting the recipients. American research on adults has shown that it can be disturbing. No adult patient likes to be reminded that his chance of life depends on another's death. But in this case, it can hardly affect Ben, and both families feel it would be right. It would be cruel to deny them this moment, and the hospital recognises that. Celia greets the Fewkes at the reception desk, and takes them all up to the ward.

I wait for them. I long to see Ben, I haven't seen him at all since the operation. But I can't. After half an hour, Celia brings the Fewkes back downstairs. Their faces are filled with happiness. Julie squeezes my hand. I think she knows how much I wanted to go with them. 'Thank you for helping to arrange this,' she says. 'He's so lovely.'

After dinner, I leave them and go back to my room. I could do with a break from all this drama. I switch on the television. I can't believe it. Professor Calne is performing a liver transplant there, in full colour, on BBC 2 – the first of a new series of *Your Life in Their Hands*. I can't tear myself away from it. This is what Ben went through. At one moment, when the patient has been disconnected from her old liver, her whole circulation seems to be draped in tubes and clips round the operating theatre. Then there were post-operative complications. It took well over a year before she'd recovered. But she did recover. I make sure I see that before I switch off, and go to sleep.

CHAPTER TEN

The story is moving almost too fast for us. Not just the fact the Fewkes have now seen Ben doing so well in intensive care – but the other letters from parents desperately asking for our help. One family had completely given up hope for their son, until they saw Ben's story. Ron and Olive Hardwick (not related at all to Debbie and Billy Hardwick) have a two-year-old boy, Andrew, with the same liver condition, biliary atresia. Ron Hardwick wrote to us from their home in Barnsley in Yorkshire:

> Andrew was born just a month before Ben. Andrew is the only little boy we know of to have this disease in Yorkshire. We had had a great deal of difficulty finding anyone in this part of the country who understood Andrew's illness, and we only finally realised what it all meant when Andrew was referred to King's College Hospital. They did an operation on his liver when he was just three months old – like Ben – but that didn't work. A transplant is now his only chance. Andrew is getting weaker now. If he is to have any chance he needs a liver transplant. Your programme has given us a ray of hope which we didn't have before. We know these operations only have a fifty-fifty chance – but for Andrew it's his only chance.

We couldn't ignore that plea – we sent a film crew to Barnsley, and they brought back enchanting pictures of Andrew and his father cuddling each other. But of course just as urgently needed in this country are the kidney transplants that can save children and adults from constant dialysis. Christopher Goacher is a beautiful baby, eighteen months old, who was born with only one kidney, and that was badly damaged. His mother, Helen, told us:

> Thanks to the fantastic team of doctors and nurses at Great Ormond Street, Christopher has been able to survive. Now his

Andrew Hardwick with his parents

Left Making friends with Ben in the hospital playroom

Top right The joy of recovery shows on Andrew's face

Below right Professor Roy Calne, whose skill has saved so many children. Celia Wight, the transplant co-ordinator at Addenbrooke's

Previous page Ben's first visit home

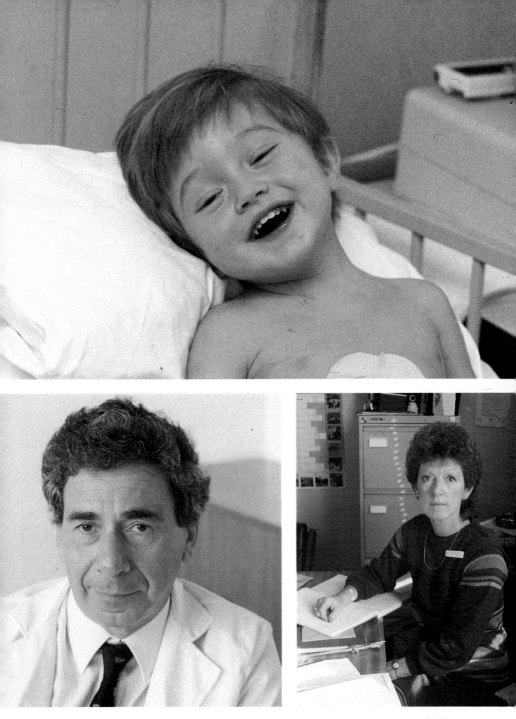

Matthew Whittaker with his mother before the operation. Back home, he plays football

Below Ben leaves hospital at last, and settles in at home (*right*)

Above '*That's Life* – can I help you?' – the crowded office that viewers never see

Left On the *That's Life* set – with his silver balloon

Right Shaun

Ben might never have had the chance to build sandcastles. . .

Below The Christmas party at Addenbrooke's

only kidney is failing fast. It has only a 6 per cent function at the moment. Doctors say they need to give him a transplant in the next six months because then his own kidney will stop working altogether.

The film crew brings back a marvellous sequence of Christopher, who adores the camera. He keeps crawling up to it and blowing raspberries straight into the lens. Thanks to these two lovely pieces of film, we can widen the story we tell this week to show just how much good organ donation can do, if it can save babies like these.

SHAUN'S DIARY

Thursday 2nd February

Mid afternoon. I call the hospital to get the latest news on Ben. Although he has been a little subdued during the day he is still happy and has been allowed to play with his toys which have been specially sterilised. I arrange for Debbie to phone me at home in the evening for a progress report.

She calls just after the nine o'clock news. I've hardly had time to say hello before she says, 'Ben's very ill. He's got a temperature of over 40° and it's getting higher. He's not able to breathe properly and is back on a ventilator. He's very, very ill. I think he might die.'

I ask her what's happened. 'He'd been fine all day. The doctors were pleased with him this morning. He was a bit quiet and he seemed to be getting a bit ratty. Then at tea-time his temperature started to go up. By 8 o'clock this evening he had become very ill. Suddenly his room was teeming with doctors and nurses. It was only then that I realised just how serious it all was. He won't die will he?'

I try to reassure her. I wonder whether it would help if I went straight up to Cambridge. But since I would be unable to enter intensive care and Debbie won't want to leave Ben's side, I feel my presence would only hinder, not help. Finally we agree that Debbie will phone me back in one hour's time.

I call Esther and give her the news. She is equally shocked. We discuss whether I should go to the hospital.

Debbie rings just about every hour through the night and keeps

109

me informed of Ben's condition. At about 2 o'clock it looks as if he can't go on fighting. His temperature is now about 40° and there is no sign of improvement. He's back on all the life-support machines he had come off after his operation. His body is packed with tubes to help him breathe, feed and take the massive doses of antibiotics and drugs. The doctors have no idea what's caused the sudden setback, but they say the only person who can now save his life is Ben himself. Once again it's up to Debbie's little soldier. The next few hours will test his will to live to the utmost.

Friday 3rd February

Just after 6 o'clock in the morning Debbie calls to say that Ben's condition has slightly improved. His temperature is down just a fraction and he seems to be responding to the antibiotics. But he is still in a critical condition. Still, like Debbie, Esther and I cling to this slender ray of hope. The atmosphere in the office this morning is extremely tense. We are all praying for Ben. Of course Esther, Gordon and I have become deeply involved in Ben's story, but I realise now that so too has every other member of the team. His sudden illness has shaken us all. Normally on script day the office resembles a bus station during rush-hour, just as crowded, busy and filled with noise. Today it seems as if everybody is tiptoeing about, waiting for the phone call we all dread.

Esther looks tired. Debbie had rung her last night, and vividly described to her how Ben was lying, eyes glazed, no flicker of recognition when she talked to him. Esther made her promise to ring through the night if there was any improvement. Then she herself was sleepless, visualising the baby's struggle to live. 'You simply cannot get so involved, it's not good for you, or for your work,' Desmond told her wearily, at dawn. At least as the day goes by Ben is still holding his own.

Esther goes down to the script room to write the show. While she is there, she takes a call from a reporter working in Cambridge. He is writing for one of the free medical papers, circulated to all doctors, subsidised by the drug company advertisements. So incredible are the questions that Esther writes them down. 'I hear the reason Ben Hardwick was able to jump the waiting list for transplants is that he is related to someone on your production team.'

'You hear what? From whom do you hear this?' 'From medical staff at Addenbrooke's.' 'Then I hope you will inform the medical staff at Addenbrooke's that Ben did not jump any waiting list. He was entered like any other patients on the records of UK Transplant. He came to our attention because his mother contacted our programme, like any other viewer. He has no relative working on the programme.' The reporter continues: 'We are told that you put great pressure on Professor Calne to perform this operation. He would not have done so otherwise.' 'What kind of gossip have you been listening to?' 'I assure you it's not gossip – my source is an eminent member of the medical staff at Addenbrooke's.' 'Then perhaps you might consider the facts. Professor Calne is internationally regarded. He puts the safety of his patients above every other consideration. We had no idea a suitable liver had been offered Ben. If Professor Calne had believed the operation should not have been performed, he would simply have turned down the offer, and nobody would have known. It was his decision, taken on medical grounds. But may I add,' Esther says, unable to prevent herself, 'that I am appalled by your questions. They reveal a malice, a professional envy, a cynicism which is quite shocking.' The reporter clearly doesn't like her either, and the conversation stops there.

She returns to the office, still shaken by that conversation. Admittedly, whatever the reporter may have claimed to her, his source could have been hospital kitchen tittle-tattle. But kitchen staff don't normally descend that low. What it sounds like is professional rivalry, from someone who very much minds the public sympathy that Ben Hardwick has aroused, and is looking for some dirt to invent. All this, when the little boy himself is fighting for his life.

The phone on Esther's desk rings again. What now? It's a reporter from the *Sun* newspaper. 'We'd like your reaction to the news.' 'What news?' Esther asks nervously. Have they heard something terrible? 'You've beaten *Coronation Street*. You're number one in the ratings. You got more than fourteen million viewers last week. Have you any comment to make?' 'It's wonderful news that one little boy can hold the attention of so many caring viewers. He's captured everyone's heart – he's responsible for the audience, not us.' Suddenly we are all aware of what enormous power for good this story has. But what enormous responsibility it brings.

SHAUN'S DIARY

Sunday 5th February

The newspapers and radio and TV have found out how ill Ben's been. Darryl and Julie Fewkes have come to London for the programme, and they're devastated. I reassure them, he really does seem to have fought off whatever the infection was. We go to the studio. Debbie has given me an up-to-date description of Ben for us to include on the air. Esther introduces the item:

ESTHER: Thank you so much for all the letters we've had from people hoping and praying Ben will continue to do well. At the moment all our prayers seem to have been answered. As we said last Sunday, Professor Calne warned us this was going to be a crucial week and, indeed, as he predicted, on Wednesday there was a slight rejection of Ben's new liver, but it was controlled by a marvellous new drug called Cyclosporin A. And Wednesday was a very good day for Debbie. She told us:

BILL: 'That afternoon, I was allowed to hold him on my lap. I had been desperate to hold him in my arms ever since the operation. When at last I could cuddle him and kiss him, it was the most marvellous moment. He was even laughing with me.'

ESTHER: But then on Thursday, he developed an infection. It was slight at first but by Thursday night, he had a very high temperature – 40°. In fact, he was very ill. But on Friday morning, Celia Wight, the transplant co-ordinator, told us:

GAVIN: 'His temperature is dropping. He is a really tough little laddie. He's a fighter. We knew that when he first arrived here and he had a series of tests. You would think that afterwards he might be a bit under the weather, but not at all. He just pushed the doctors out of the way, marched over to his toys and started playing with them. Which is terrific, of course.'

ESTHER: And in fact, his temperature went right back to normal, which was a relief to everyone, as you can imagine. Well, tonight just before the programme, we spoke to Debbie

112

and she said he is doing very well – since lunch-time, he has eaten two portions of ice cream, and Weetabix which seems to be his favourite, and chocolate milk and yoghourt. He has been sitting on a high chair, he's been sitting on Debbie's lap, he has been showing-off, being very naughty, laughing and saying 'No' a lot. Isn't it marvellous news?

It's been a very eventful week for Mr and Mrs Fewkes too. You remember it was when their baby Matthew tragically died that they decided to donate his liver, to try and save Ben. Last Sunday, they told us how they prayed for Ben and how much they wanted to meet Debbie and Ben. Well, this week, with their daughter Vicky, they met Debbie. Debbie told us:

BILL: 'We spent Tuesday afternoon together. It was incredible – as soon as I met them, I realised how much we had in common. We chatted for ages about Ben and Matthew and we found out that they had been born only a couple of days apart. We swopped photographs. Matthew was lovely – blond hair and dark eyes. I'll keep the picture for ever.'

ESTHER: Well, Mr and Mrs Fewkes are here with us this evening. That meeting must have meant an awful lot to you, did it?

JULIE: Yes, ever since the transplant took place, I've wanted to meet Ben and his family. Now we have. They are wonderful people. We're going to keep in touch.

ESTHER: What did you talk to Debbie about?

JULIE: We had a lot of things in common, with Matthew, Ben . . .

ESTHER: They were almost the same age, weren't they?

JULIE: Yes, there were a few days between them.

ESTHER: And you swopped pictures, as we've heard?

JULIE: Yes, we've got a lovely picture of Ben. We're going to put it in between Vicky and Matthew.

ESTHER: That's lovely. Now you said last week how much you were longing to see Ben and that in fact has happened – tell us about that.

JULIE: Yes, on Tuesday evening we went to the intensive care unit. We couldn't go in, we could just look through the window and when he saw us, he pointed and waved to us.

ESTHER: Can I ask you one other thing: I think what worries a lot of doctors, and may worry a lot of people watching, is that it was at your moment of greatest tragedy, when your own little boy was going to die, that Dr Jardine asked your permission for him to be used as a donor. Did that question hurt you? Did it distress you?

JULIE: Not any more than we already were. We were distressed – I don't think anybody could be more distressed than when their baby dies. It helped us a lot to know that he might somehow help to save Ben's life.

ESTHER: What do you think, Darryl?

DARRYL: Well, we hoped it would help. We knew we had lost our son, and we hoped . . . it was just like bringing a new life back into the world. We would do it again, if asked.

ESTHER: Thank you so much. Of course, in a way, the remarkable thing about you both is that, at the moment of your own greatest tragedy, you were able to think about saving another life. It is much easier for most of us to make this kind of decision quietly, now, when it is not literally a matter of life and death. But perhaps that might mean having some system of donor cards, or storing our names as potential donors on a computer. And, indeed, that's what a great many of our viewers letters have been about. Because, if someone carries a card, or places their name on record, on a computer, doctors don't feel so intrusive or callous if they ask permission to use them as donors. The people who co-ordinate transplants in this country are UK Transplant in Bristol. Their administrator, Peter Brooman, told us:

GAVIN: 'Doctors tend to feel that it is hard and distressing enough to have to say to relatives "I'm sorry, we can't save your relative's life", let alone having to ask whether they can be used as donors. There is a terrible shortage now of kidneys and livers and all transplant organs and it is mainly caused by the reluctance of doctors and nurses to ask relatives of someone who is dying. But if people think about it now, and not when they're in the middle of a tragedy, if doctors didn't think that by asking these questions, they would create a terrible shock, then I'm sure they would have much more confidence. There is no doubt that enough adult and child donors could be found. The shortage is because doctors and nurses are afraid. What you have shown is that they needn't be.'

ESTHER: Well, of course, in fact what Mr and Mrs Fewkes have shown is that they needn't be. Among the letters we've had this week have been some more tragic cases, some more children like Ben, who are desperate for transplants. One letter was from Ron Hardwick – he's no relation of Ben's – he lives in Barnsley. His son Andrew, who is two months older than Ben, is suffering from the same liver disease. As you can see from his picture, he is a lovely baby but, like Ben, they say he's living on borrowed time. Mr Hardwick told us:

BILL: 'Andrew is getting weaker now. If he is to have any chance, he needs a liver transplant. Your programme has given us a ray of hope which we didn't have before. We know these operations only have a fifty-fifty chance but for our Andrew, it's the only chance.'

ESTHER: And, of course, not only liver donors are badly needed. We had another letter from Helen Goacher, who lives in Horsham in Sussex and she said:

MICHAEL: 'My baby Christopher was born with only one kidney and that was not properly formed. Now, it's failing fast. It has only a 6 per cent function and, at the moment, doctors say that they need to give him a transplant in the next six months, because then his own kidney will stop working altogether.'

115

ESTHER: Another lovely baby, as you see, and he seems to have a strong desire to become a cameraman. But if Christopher doesn't get a transplant, he's going to need dialysis three days a week for the rest of his life, which is difficult and expensive treatment. Whereas a kidney transplant has a very high success rate and, in fact, it is cheaper than dialysis. The main thing preventing the operation on the nearly three thousand people who now need kidney transplants, is the shortage of donors. And that could be resolved, as our viewer said, in her letter:

GAVIN: 'Please, parents, be brave and offer and doctors, be brave and ask.'

ESTHER: Mrs Fewkes, from your own experience, you would agree with that?

JULIE AND DARRYL: Yes, very much so.

ESTHER: Thank you Mr and Mrs Fewkes so much for coming to tell us what you feel about this. Our viewers have asked us to send you their good wishes for the future.

CHAPTER ELEVEN

SHAUN'S DIARY

Tuesday 7th February

The BBC has an amiable way of making sure you don't get too self-important. Just as Ben's story develops dramatically, the viewers join us in millions, we reach number one in the ratings, they take us off the air to make way for Cruft's Dog Show. It quite restores our sense of perspective to realise that the BBC rates a ringful of prize pooches higher than us.

My sense of perspective is heightened still further as I sit at home this evening and realise how cold the flat is. Oddly enough, the cooker seems to be on the blink too. Then I notice the stack of brown envelopes piled on the mantelpiece. Bills. Final demands. I haven't had time even to open them in the last two months. We've been cut off. Gas, electricity, the lot. What an achievement for a researcher on a consumer programme. In desperation I move out of the flat, and go to stay with a friend.

Wednesday 8th February

Debbie rings the office. Wonderful news – they've moved Ben out of intensive care into his own room on the children's ward. Still the danger of infection, of course, so very limited visiting, and Ben is still in isolation, but it's a real step forward. Les and I travel to Cambridge to see if he can get any new photographs of Ben. He can't. We haven't been allowed to take any since the operation, and the hospital certainly isn't changing its mind now. Les argues, pleads, and then collapses into a sulk. I decide I'd better leave him alone to get over it. He disappears into the grounds and I presume he's sitting under some bush somewhere, grinding his teeth. Not at all. An hour later he's back, beaming with pleasure, with a small box in his hands. He passes the box over to Debbie. 'This is for you,' he says, in a syrupy voice. It's a camera, which she can use, which takes pictures good enough for us to use on the screen. His voice loses its syrup. 'The so-and-sos may not let me in, but they'll let you in, and if you want to take pictures, then they can't stop you. If you want to, you can even let us show a few on television. But of course, that's up to you, Debs.' She's thrilled, and later, for obvious reasons, so are we when she lets us have a marvellous picture she's taken of Ben and teddy bear, asleep in his cot in his new room. Grudgingly Les has to admit that she may not be a professional but it's the best picture of Ben so far. We enlarge it, and Bob Marsland, our director, sticks it up on our office wall. Everyone just likes looking at it.

Friday 10th February

Esther rings from Manchester. She's been doing street interviews and is showered with presents for Ben. People rush into shops and come out with cuddly toys for him. One thin little lady takes out a battered wallet and pulls a pound note out of it. 'Take it for the little boy,' she says. Esther looks over her shoulder. There is no other money in the wallet – it's the woman's last pound note. The little lady disappears into the crowd again.

A wonderful letter has arrived in the office:

> I am a sister working on the renal transplant unit at St Mary's Hospital in Paddington. We watched your two programmes on the lack of donor organs with great interest and as a direct result of this we had two offers of donor kidneys over the weekend of 27th January. We transplanted two patients who were on dialysis and both are doing well.
>
> Prior to this we had no offers of kidneys for four months so we were delighted to see the problems being handled so well on your programme. One of the donor's relatives had seen your programme and offered the organs for transplantation before they had been approached by any doctors, so your acknowledgement of the problem seems to have made the general public and medical staff more aware of this problem.
>
> Thanks again, you have made two renal patients very happy.

Sunday 12th February

Esther watches Cruft's go out in our slot, her teeth snarling like a Dobermann pinscher. If only the judges could have seen her, she would certainly have won a prize for ferocity. She claims she enjoys Cruft's, particularly the judges, who are nearly all female, and while they are walking the dogs, appear from the waist down only, displaying a truly British collection of tweed skirts and brogue shoes. I suggest *That's Life* would improve if she appeared the same way. She makes a reply which would bar her from the Kennel Club for life.

Monday 13th February

The morning is absolutely frantic. Sir John Biggs-Davison and Richard Tracey, boths MPs, have been trying to reach either Esther or me to discuss transplant surgery. Sir John has secured a debate on transplant surgery in the House of Commons this afternoon and having been prompted by the *That's Life* coverage on Ben Hardwick he wants to use our material.

I finally catch up with Sir John at lunchtime. He'd be grateful for any information we can supply, so I gather together a batch of the countless letters we have received from viewers, many of them from relatives of donors, or from parents who have lost a child and desperately wish that they had been asked if their child could be a donor. Richard Tracey wants exactly the same information and I arrange for another batch of letters to go to him.

In the afternoon I go over to Westminster to hear the debate. Sir John begins by talking about the present number of kidney transplants – 1160 in 1983. He points out that this still leaves 2400 patients awaiting a transplant. He then takes up the subject of liver transplants in children. He praises the *That's Life* coverage of Ben Hardwick, and comments:

> The huge public response to the *That's Life* programme has shown that many relatives felt that the saving of another's life or health by a transplant gave, or might have given, solace to their grief. There were those who only wished that they had been asked. A common reaction is to say, 'I should have felt that he had not died for nothing.'

The debate soon develops into a discussion of the various ways the supply of organs for transplants can be increased. One scheme which comes under considerable scrutiny is the one referred to as 'opting-out'.

At present we all 'opt in'. Opting-in means that if you want your organs to be used for transplant surgery after your death, you have to register your consent on a donor card. Your signature therefore indicates to the medical staff who find it in the event of your death that you have given your consent. In other countries like Sweden and France there is a system of opting-out. There medical staff can assume that you have consented to allow your organs to be used for transplant surgery in the event of your death unless you have signed a card to the contrary. The system is based on the assumption that everyone wishes to be a donor unless he or she has registered an objection, has literally opted out.

During the debate, John Patten, the Under-Secretary of State for Health and Social Security, announces that in the near future the government is going to re-launch a 'publicity campaign to try to increase the awareness of the general public of the need to carry an organ donor card'. The government is enlisting the help of professional and commercial groups, charitable and voluntary organisations and community groups.

He briefly discusses the opting-out scheme. He feels that the idea is not yet appropriate for Britain. First, because of possible reluctance by doctors; second, because:

> there is evidence to suggest that people are quite strongly opposed to the idea of an opting-out system, whether rightly or wrongly I am not saying; I am not giving an opinion. Our most recent public opinion polls still show a continuing opposition to opting-out. That may mean that we have failed in the task of education.

Is he right? Are people really opposed to an idea like this? Certainly he seems to have statistical evidence to support his claim that public opinion is against it – although he never actually produces the opinion poll or mentions that it was carried out in 1979.

At the end of the debate Richard Tracey delivers a very moving tribute to the courage of Debbie Hardwick in her fight for a life for Ben. To a chamberful of MPs he says:

One can understand the sheer horror felt by that young mother, then aged 20, when she realised that her child was likely to die. She is a most persistent and dedicated mother, to whom I pay tribute.

He goes on to describe Debbie's plight and how she had come to the BBC for help. He retells the story of the Nottingham anaesthetist who had been told by his wife that a little boy needed a transplant and how it happened that in an operation in the hospital that week a little boy had suffered heart failure – Matthew Fewkes.

. . . the parents of the child, Matthew Fewkes . . . were only too happy to say that if their child died – unfortunately he did in the following few days – his liver could be donated to save Ben Hardwick. That rounds off a wonderful story of parental dedication, and great feeling by the parents in Nottingham.

At the end of his speech, Richard Tracey reads out a number of letters we have received. The MPs seem quite spellbound by them – examples of such courage and generosity. Everyone listens with great intensity.

We are delighted that the Hardwicks and the Fewkes have been given the tributes they so richly deserve. The significance of the debate cannot be underestimated – Parliament is now discussing the question of transplant surgery, particularly how to increase the number of donors. Ben Hardwick's fight for life has already achieved far more than anyone could have ever imagined.

CHAPTER TWELVE

The hospital have told us that when Ben is moved out of intensive care into his own room, we can film him there. We have to guarantee that we will supply some of our footage to BBC News, and to Independent Television News. All this has been painstakingly negotiated by Gordon over the last week. Press photographers have also been invited in to take their first pictures of Ben for the papers.

On Wednesday, Esther, Shaun and Martin O'Collins, our film director, drive to Cambridge. We stop on the way to buy some presents for Ben – a wooden chicken that clucks when it's pulled along and, remembering how Ben loves bubbles, a little pot of bubble liquid.

We arrive in the sunny, cheerful children's ward. A white gown has been provided for Esther, and one for each of the crew who has to enter Ben's room. The risk of infection is still high – Ben is on high dosages of anti-rejection drugs, which suppress his own immune system, so now a mild virus, even chicken-pox, could kill him. Esther has just come from a house filled with toddlers, all of them harbouring nameless bugs. She can't bear to think about it. She determines to stay well away from Ben, just in case.

Martin describes to the crew how he wants the scene to be covered. Only the cameraman will go into the room with Esther. While they are setting up the equipment, Esther talks to the nurses. A woman comes up to Esther. 'Would it be possible to have an autograph for my son?' 'Of course,' says Esther, searching wildly for a pen and failing to find one. A nurse kindly lends her one. Shaun whispers to Esther, 'That boy is Matthew Whittaker. Do you remember, his parents wrote to us because he's a medical miracle – he's got biliary atresia, and was expected to die at two, but he's managed to survive. He's 11 now. He's had countless operations and blood transfusions, but he has an amazing will to live.

Because they saw the programme his parents wrote to Professor Calne to see if a transplant would be possible. I wonder if that's why he's here. I bet they're doing the preliminary tests, in case another donor can be found.'

Esther signs Matthew's book, and grins at him. He grins shyly back. He has the characteristic thin arms, and slightly bloated stomach caused by liver disease. His smile etches itself on Esther's memory. If only . . . she thinks. It seems dangerous even to put the hope into words, but once again her mind won't let it drop. The last time she dared hope, Ben had his transplant. Is it a crime to hope? She glances at Shaun. Quite clearly he is thinking exactly the same. They both look at Matthew's mother, Mrs Whittaker. She puts a protective arm round Matthew and they walk away down the ward. What can those last eleven years have been like for that family?

The crew is ready. The first sequence won't involve Esther. Billy Hardwick has the pot of bubble liquid, and he and Debbie start to blow bubbles for Ben. It's Esther's first glimpse of Ben, as she peeps through the door at him. No wonder he has had such an effect on everyone who's seen him – a mop of soft brown hair, eyes bright blue, and fringed with heavy eyelashes – the vivid flash of a smile as the bubbles break round his fingers. 'More,' he commands his father. Billy blows a stream of bubbles at him. Ben lets out a deep chuckle. It's the scene that will feature in both news bulletins that weekend, BBC and ITV. Ben, the star, couldn't care less. He bats a bubble onto his mother's cheek and chuckles again. His arms and legs are painfully thin, delicate as twigs. He has a portable drip attached to one arm, to carry the drugs he needs. His tummy is still swaddled with bandages. But he is alive, very much alive.

Ben is lifted on to his cot, and Professor Calne arrives. Esther greets him cautiously – hoping he won't mind her being so close to his precious patient. He motions her even closer to Ben, and pulls out a tiny camera. 'Must have a picture of you two together,' he says. She grabs an opportunity. 'May we have a picture of you with Ben?' she asks. Professor Calne shakes his head. 'No, not yet. I'll talk to you the day Ben goes home.' They nod at each other. 'See you later,' Professor Calne says, and he's gone, as quickly and unexpectedly as he'd arrived.

But his confidence is catching. Esther leans over the side of Ben's cot with a glove puppet he's been given. Ben looks doubtfully at her. The puppet squeaks at him – 'Can I have a drink please Ben?' He offers the puppet his bottle of juice. The puppet pretends to suck noisily then gets hiccups. Ben roars with laughter. The cameraman has sneaked up behind Esther's shoulder and is filming Ben's jokes. Esther is spellbound – doesn't want to stop the game. Neither does Ben. The puppet starts to overact – getting hiccups, falling over drunk. Ben laughs and goes on feeding him from the bottle. For five minutes they play together.

Esther remembers a moment from the previous summer. She and her family had spent the day with their friend Cyril Fletcher, and his wife Betty Astell, who lived then in a beautiful village in Sussex. Behind their house there was a field filled with clovers and long-stemmed buttercups. Esther's children romped through the field, almost hidden in golden flowers, the sunshine glowing on their hair. Esther will always remember her children's happiness on that long summer day in Sussex. Now another thought invades her mind. Suppose this summer Ben, too, can run through a field of buttercups. She tries to fight the thought. It won't disappear. It becomes a constant dream for her over the next few months – if only Ben can have the sunshine, the freedom, the sheer fun that her own children enjoy.

Debbie lifts Ben onto her lap, and Esther starts the interview.

ESTHER: It is four weeks now since he had his operation. How have those four weeks been for you?

DEBBIE: Awful really. You can't relax yet. We haven't ever relaxed and said 'That's it, we have got it all done.' We daren't look too far forward. We know there are potential hurdles yet, still hurdles to come.

ESTHER: What are the worst risks for him now?

DEBBIE: I think infection is the worst, and rejection.

ESTHER: Have you asked the doctors what effect this enormous operation might have on Ben later in life?

DEBBIE: No, I haven't. I would like to know, because he has been very frightened and I wonder if he will always remember it.

124

ESTHER: When was he frightened?

DEBBIE: When he was in intensive care, he was absolutely terrified for a couple of days. He was really, really frightened. And sometimes even now he will get the odd day when you can see the fear in his eyes.

ESTHER: What is he frightened of?

DEBBIE: Just anybody who comes near him, anybody he doesn't know. He automatically thinks they are going to do something to him. The fear is awful to see – he cries like a little dog sometimes. Hopefully he will forget it.

ESTHER: Does he laugh as well?

DEBBIE: Yes, it is more laughter than anything else now, since yesterday. Yesterday we had a lovely day. He was really happy. He had me running around all over the room, picking things up for him as he was throwing them.

ESTHER: Professor Calne says that his chances of living a year now are 70 per cent.

DEBBIE: That is lovely. But I can't let myself relax, because I can't be knocked over again. When he was a year old we hoped it was all going to be okay. Then we were told he'd die. So we can't relax now, because I couldn't take that sudden knock once again.

ESTHER: How soon do you think it will be before you dare think of the future?

DEBBIE: I don't know. When he goes home I suppose. I do have a sneaky view of it sometimes. I think that maybe he will go to school some day, and that sort of thing. But I try not to.

ESTHER: Suppose he doesn't pull through?

DEBBIE: If I lost Ben, he wouldn't have lived for nothing. He has done something in his small life. He has achieved something.

The interview reveals very clearly that Debbie is not living in a fool's paradise. She knows the risks, she understands that Ben may still die. We know it too. From time to time, worried BBC bosses have reminded us, 'You realise the child may die. What then? Now that you have built so much hope round him, what will you do if he dies?' Of course we have considered the possibility. The fear is very seldom out of our minds. We almost get the feeling there are people who think we should never have embarked on this story, because the risks are so great. And yet, little Ben has saved lives already. Donors have been found, relatives have consented to transplants, because Ben has shown their value, demonstrated the crying need for them. Debbie is right, he has already achieved so much in his small life.

Shaun and Esther arrange to have lunch with Professor Calne. On the way, they shower him with questions. They tell him about letters they've received from anti-vivisectionists, claiming that transplant surgery involves needless experimentation on animals. Calne sighs. Sadly there is no other way to test new drugs, like cyclosporin. But this drug has been crucial in saving children's lives. All that existed previously to combat rejection of an implanted organ were steroids. Steroids have a 'humpty dumpty' effect on children if they are used too long – stunting growth and causing them to bloat. That is why Professor Calne did not perform transplants on children until the advent of cyclosporin. 'The animal lobby nearly killed one of my technicians,' he told them. 'They sent a bomb to the laboratory.' Then he told them how his staff care for the animals they have to use in the vital tests, avoiding all suffering as far as they possibly can. Clearly he would use other methods, if he could. If that bomb had reached its target, how many other human lives would have been lost, all the patients who owe their survival to Calne's skill.

He tells them that since Ben's transplant he has begun to receive letters from doctors all over the country, and from the families of desperately ill children. 'I can't help them,' he says. 'There still aren't the donors.'

At lunch he orders devilled kidneys. Esther and Shaun watch, fascinated, as he spears a slice of kidney on his fork. 'Delicious, you should try them,' he suggests, wickedly. He knows why they have both chosen fish.

Esther asks him how he can work this punishing schedule, oper-ating for eight hours on end, all through the night, then starting again the next morning. He looks vaguely at her – it's clearly become a way of life for him.

Esther asks the most difficult question. Does he realise that the children who are coming forward for transplants have not been referred to him by King's, the recognised centre for treating children with liver disease? They have found their own way to him, like Debbie, via America. Or like the other Hardwick family, and the Whittakers, prompted by our programme. Sharon Knight on the other hand has been recommended to send Gemma, her little daughter, to America for a transplant. She phoned Esther to try and persuade Debbie to do the same. Sharon had been told the medical expertise doesn't exist in Britain. Who has told her this? Professor Calne seems surprised. 'I work very closely with the team at King's,' he says. 'Their consultants are in charge of all the post-operative drug treatment for liver transplants on adults. I can't imagine that they don't know the level of skill we have here, and our success rate.'

Esther puts Sharon Knight's question to him. 'Is it harder to operate on children? Is that a special skill that only exists in America?' 'No, in fact this operation is easier on children than on adults.' We change the subject. But when it comes to allocating the money that has come in so generously to help save children like Ben, some of the fund is used to finance a doctor's post, a joint paediatric fellowship, working at both centres of excellence, King's in London, and Addenbrooke's in Cambridge, to act as a bridge between them. If there has been a curious lack of referrals in the past, this should ease the situation in the future.

We discuss Monday's debate in Parliament – Calne believes that the donor-card system in the end will have to be replaced by an opting-out method, with all the safeguards to make sure that an individual's right to opt out is protected. And, indeed, that a family's right to decide to refuse to allow transplantation is also protected. 'But whatever the system,' he says, 'it must always depend on the goodwill of the medical profession. I think people know now how crucial these organs are – but without doctors in intensive care asking the right question, and making transplantation possible, we can achieve nothing.'

That afternoon, we have decided to conduct our own tiny test of

127

public opinion, in the streets of Cambridge. The Minister for Health has stated his belief that most people would be against the opting-out system, but he has no up-to-date research to prove his point. We suspect he may be wrong. Esther stops twenty-five people and asks their views. Twenty-three of them are in favour of an opting-out system – they find it less morbid, and more dependable than signing a donor card and remembering to carry it always. One person says he would not want ever to be used as a donor. But out of twenty-four people who say they would wish to be used as donors, if possible, after death, only one person actually carries a card. She is a young woman, pushing a baby in a pram. She tells Esther, 'My husband carries a card as well. I feel, if you are going to die, what is the point of letting your body rot in the ground or get burned, when somebody else could make use of transplants.' Twenty-three other people in Esther's tiny survey agree with her, but as they don't carry cards, no one would know. In an opt-out system, the card would not be necessary. It would only be necessary for the people who object, to register their objection.

Back at the office the next day, Gordon, Esther and Shaun discuss whether this tiny unofficial poll could be conducted nationally. We commission MORI to conduct one, to see how public opinion has been affected, if at all, by Ben's story.

Ben himself grows stronger daily, he is standing in his cot now, calling for his mum, and feeding himself roast beef and mash.

SHAUN'S DIARY

Monday 20th February

Every newspaper carries a story and photograph of Ben on their front page. The *Daily Mirror* uses the headline BRAVO BEN and shows him with a paper hat on his head; inside on the centre pages are more pictures of Ben and a report on his progress with the heading MY LITTLE HERO. The *Guardian* has a picture of Debbie cuddling Ben. The *Mail* has him feeding himself. The headline runs BRAVE BEN TASTES SWEET LIFE. The *Sun* uses quotes from *That's Life* in its story – MY FIGHT TO GIVE LIFE TO DARLING BEN – and has another picture of Debbie and Ben cuddling together. The *Daily Telegraph* use virtually the same photograph, and *The Times* and *Daily Express* have a photo of Ben and his paper hat. The *Daily Star* devotes two pages to Ben, including a report by Charles Langley, their excellent medical correspondent. Their front page shows a close-up of Ben with the headline THIS IS LIFE.

Tuesday 21st February

In contrast to yesterday's newspapers, a shock of cold water pours over us – a story by the freebie medical publication who've been so unpleasant to Esther. They call the Ben case 'a disastrous precedent' – in spite of Esther's assurances they say we 'hastened' the operation. They criticise it because they say the risks are still too high – and 'a few well-publicised failures could undermine public confidence and set the programme back years'.

Without donors, the child liver transplant programme was not happening at all in this country, a simple fact they seem to overlook. They don't accept Professor Calne's predictions of the potential success of his operations. They say we have created a demand for transplants that could not possibly be met. And they have their cake as well as eating it by saying that when we go away, the effect of our coverage will go away too, and the rate of donors will slump.

Basically they say we were wrong to talk about Ben, and we'll be wrong when we stop talking about Ben. It's heart-warming stuff.

I'm furious, because apart from that brief conversation with Esther they haven't contacted us at all to see the kind of letters we've had. They've evidently made up their minds on their angle, and be blowed to the facts. Esther is less angry. She'd known from the tone of their conversation with her what to expect, and she was only glad she was able to contradict some of the scandal they'd been fed.

Still, what the hell. The other newspapers have treated the story very well, and the Hardwicks and the Fewkes have been heartened by the way people are coming up to them, saying how inspired they've been by the story and, above all, wishing Ben well.

Wednesday 22 February

The Department of Health is launching a new, multi-organ donor card, to replace the old kidney donor card. It's pure coincidence that this should happen now, right in the middle of the Ben story, but of course it means the press turn out in force. Norman Fowler, the Secretary of State for Social Services, and John Patten are both there. So are several eminent transplant surgeons (not Professor Calne), most of them growling under their breath. We hear one complaining loudly, 'It won't work. These cards never work. A body gets picked up in the road and rushed into intensive care. Who's going to scrabble around in the gutter trying to find out where a handbag or a wallet has landed? Nobody bothers to look for a donor card – not in reality. It's a nonsense.' Put like that, the card does seem a bit impractical. Some of our viewers have written to suggest that people who want to be donors should wear a special tattoo, or bracelet. We have dismissed the idea as loony, but maybe they have a point.

Nevertheless, I see Esther filling in one of the new cards and putting it carefully in her wallet. She's never carried one before – the thought of it used to frighten her.

A man from the Kidney Patients' Association come up to tell us the weekly rate of kidney donations has doubled since our first story about Ben.

A gentleman from UK Transplant introduces himself to us. 'We should be very angry with you,' he says. 'Ben should have got his liver through us, not through you. Why didn't the donor hospital consult us? We could have told them exactly what was needed.' He's right of course. We tell him about the consultant from Scotland who had never heard of UK Transplant. Shouldn't the Ministry make sure these lines of communication are known about, and used properly?

On cue a senior woman doctor, a civil servant from the Ministry, joins us. We start talking about the opt-out system. 'I'm agin it,' she declares roundly. 'If a form came through the front door asking you to register your objections if you don't want to be used as a donor, and it landed on my gaga old mother's mat, she wouldn't make head nor tail of it. Probably frighten her to death.' On that basis, her gaga old mother would have prevented the introduction of VAT. The lady is clearly not at all keen on the whole subject of transplantation. Equally clearly, she is a very influential person in the Ministry. On the way home we realise her gaga old mother is unlikely to be asked to donate any organs anyway. It's the kind of reply you always think of too late.

130

Thursday 23rd February

The results of the MORI poll come through. We have been very nervous of this moment. Perhaps it would reveal that the country is implacably opposed to the idea of becoming donors.

The first question MORI has asked is whether people would be prepared to donate organs after their death, to save other people. 13 per cent said they didn't know. 9 per cent said no, they wouldn't. 77 per cent said yes, they would be prepared to be donors. More than three-quarters of the survey.

Then they asked about carrying donor cards, cards which have been available for the last thirteen years. Only 11 per cent said they carried them. Nine out of ten people don't carry donor cards. How then would doctors know that many of them would want to be used as donors?

Then MORI turned to the opt-out system. 'In certain other countries,' they said, 'there is a system whereby everyone's organs can be used for transplants after they die, unless they have recorded an objection. Relatives are still asked for their agreement for the organs to be used, and no organs are used from anyone who has objected. Would you be in favour, or opposed to a similar system being adopted in Britain?'

6 per cent didn't know. 23 per cent were against opting out. 71 per cent of people said they would be in favour of this scheme. More than we'd ever expected, even though Esther's tiny sample of opinion in Cambridge had shown that people are favourably inclined to the whole subject of transplantation.

Norman Fowler, answering a question from Esther at the press conference, had said that if there were to be a massive swing in favour of the opt-out scheme, government and parliament would have to take note of it. Is this what he calls a massive swing? Probably not. But obviously we will report this fascinating result, in Sunday's programme.

That afternoon, a call comes into the office from a South London newspaper. They have just interviewed a woman whose little boy was killed in a tragic accident. He was a great fan of Ben Hardwick, and watched every programme about him. When he died, his mother asked the doctors if he could be used as a donor. Esther asks

131

Shaun to talk to the mother. Would she be prepared to give us an interview? Shaun reports back. She will be interviewed. What she says is wonderful, moving, strongly felt, deeply courageous.

Gordon's mother is very ill – he has had to leave London to look after her. Esther decides to book a film crew, and asks the mother, Rose Morrison, to meet her in Lime Grove studios the next morning.

She arrives early on Friday morning. Rose has a strong, open face, blonde hair, a locket round her neck with a picture of a boy. Her dead son, Jason. Esther and Rose sit down together. The camera rolls, Esther asks Rose to tell her story. Jason died less than a week ago, falling from a high wall where he was playing. Rose speaks simply and clearly, with no tears. She has exhausted her tears. After ten minutes, the roll of film has finished. Esther tries to speak, to ask Rose to stop for a second while they put on a fresh roll of film. She finds she can't speak, instead, tears well up in her eyes. The electrician sitting behind the lights is in tears. Nobody can speak.

If ever a woman proves Professor Calne's beliefs, this mother does. No doctor has asked if they can use Jason as a donor, the impulse comes from her. Far from being a source of additional grief, she finds it a great comfort – her sporty little boy, brave, athletic, compassionate in his deep interest in baby Ben has now saved three lives. They have been able to use his kidneys and his heart. After the operation, Jason looks peaceful and untouched. His schoolboy friends have visited him in the chapel of rest. Rose describes the comfort it gives her, knowing his strong little heart is still at work, saving another life.

Gordon returns to the office. Esther describes the interview to him. He is unconvinced that they should run it in the programme. The bosses are beginning to grumble – aren't we devoting too much time to this story. Isn't it time we moved on? We are moving on – with our MORI poll, and reporting the launch of the new donor card. But should we really run another interview with a bereaved parent?

Esther agrees with him, in theory. But Rose Morrison is special. She asks Gordon to come and listen to the recording of the interview. Together they go to a listening booth, and play the tape. Gordon's eyes brim with tears. Rose makes the argument so powerfully. At the end of the recording there is no discussion. Gordon simply outlines the points he thinks she makes most powerfully. Esther goes to the script room, to work out the item, including Rose. Esther will have to edit the film itself on Saturday – officially her only day off. Ben is becoming a full-time job. Thank heavens, as an experienced programme-maker himself, Desmond understands the reasons for Esther's long absences.

Sunday's programme gives a progress report on Ben, the results of the press conference and the MORI poll, and then shows the interview with Rose Morrison.

ROSE: I asked the doctors everything. I asked them if Jason was in any pain, and they explained every detail to me. And they explained . . . Jason will be taken to the theatre and will be operated on like a normal person, and a proper operation was performed. Jason didn't feel anything. And, they said to me the moment they took Jason's heart, Jason was dead. But you know he isn't dead, because his heart's still working. So I know that he isn't dead, he's still fighting for somebody else now. And it's made me feel so happy. Part of me is so sad, but the other part feels so happy. There aren't words to explain how I feel. I've even spoken to the vicar and asked, 'Why should a part of me feel happy?' The vicar said, 'Because you've done what Jason wanted you to do.' I know I won't have him again and I know he'll never come home, but I know that Jason is still fighting out there. And he really did fight, right until the end. He's given me so much courage. It's only what Jason's given me, you know. I've got so much courage now, so much hope. I've been to see Jason. He looked so peaceful, and he's telling me, 'Thank you, Mum, you've done what I wanted you to do.

ESTHER: What happened to his heart and his kidneys?

ROSE: Jason's heart was rushed to Harefield and it was given to a fifty-year-old man. They felt that this man needed a young strong heart, so that's why they picked Jason. And a twenty-year-old boy was having one of his kidneys. His other kidney

133

was rushed to King's College Hospital where a sixteen-year-old girl was waiting for a transplant. Jason was such a lovely boy in every respect and now, you know, his life's not been a complete waste. In that locket is a picture of Jason, he looks beautiful and I'll never ever forget him . . . I really will miss him.

(Film ends)

ESTHER: Well, there's nothing we can say listening to such courage except to thank Rose Morrison for telling us Jason's story. She and Jason have saved three lives, and so, in a way, has Ben, who began the story. Since he appeared on our programme we've been told that the weekly rate of kidney donors has doubled. And we're delighted to say that Ben, who's achieved so much for other people, is also doing very well himself.

MICHAEL: This week, for the first time since his liver transplant, he walked to the door of his hospital room. He's clearly thinking of leaving.

ESTHER: Sadly we have to leave you, too, now. So, till next week, goodnight.

In Cambridge, Celia Wight, Addenbrooke's transplant co-ordinator, watches the programme with her husband. He has seen her, travelling round the region, wearily trying to persuade staff in intensive care units that they can, they must, put this question to bereaved families. As Rose finishes, he turns to Celia. 'She's put your points better than any doctor, or any nurse, ever could. You couldn't ask for a more valuable piece of film to help your work.' Now that filmed interview with Rose Morrison is being used to train other transplant co-ordinators and to show staff in intensive care units how parents can take the initiative – and how organ donation can ease the immediate pain of bereavement. Jason's memory lives on – who knows how many more lives he may still be saving, by his example.

CHAPTER THIRTEEN

SHAUN'S DIARY

Monday 27th February

On Friday the front page of the *Daily Express* was half-filled with a picture of Gemma Knight, about to fly to Pittsburgh for her liver transplant operation. We all send her love, and good luck. We all hope it won't be necessary for any other children to be flown to America – Matthew Whittaker and little Andrew Hardwick are always in our thoughts. Time is running out for them, too.

Then, just before lunch, Debbie calls. She can hardly speak for joy. 'It's Ben. He's standing nine feet away from me, in the reception of the hospital. He's so happy to be out of his intensive care room. I'm so happy. It's wonderful. He's been walking everywhere with me. Professor Calne thinks the time has come for him to get out in the air and out of his special room. We'll have to be very careful of course but can you believe it? The liver's fine. He's still on antibiotics and he has to carry round a little pack on his back which has his drugs in it. But he's so happy.' It's a big step, to allow Ben to mix with the other children in the hospital. Clearly he's getting stronger every day.

Sunday 4th March

We have a marvellous film sequence of Ben playing on a rocking horse. He gazes round the hospital playroom with delight, his eyes shine. When he's happy, he seems to light up with such joy, such a sense of fun – and yet he is still delicate.

Just before we record the programme, Debbie rings me with fresh news. I run to find Esther and Gordon. Matthew Whittaker's mother, Irene, wants to speak to them. It's not the ideal time, when the last-minute cuts for time and word checks are being made. But they both run to the phone. She tells them that they have been called to Addenbrooke's that afternoon – a donor has been found for Matthew. 'They want to perform the transplant tonight. We're waiting now for the operation to begin.' We tell her we're thinking of her, send our love to Matthew, all the inadequate things you say when you know that the next few hours will decide whether he lives or dies. She asks us to keep the news secret. Of course we agree.

Monday 5th March

As far as they can tell, the operation is a success. But Matthew's life is still in the balance. It will be for the next few weeks and months.

Friday 9th March

All this time, money has been pouring into the office. We've never asked for it, but by every post it arrives. Milkmen in Finchley are organising a sponsored walk, and hope to raise £1000 or more. Children at a primary school in Gateshead are holding a raffle and hope to raise about £120. Pupils in Halifax have held a 'no school uniform day' – they all had to pay 10 pence not to wear uniform and they sent the whole amount to the Ben fund – £70. There have been massive toddler marathons, one in Hull, one in Reigate. Between them they raise £9000. Our own team – Michael Groth, Bill Buckley and Jo Monro – have formed a group called 'Dangerous Toys' and held a series of charity concerts. We have told viewers that the money will be used to save the lives of children like Ben. Gordon decides he must hire a new researcher, Catherine Boyd, to discover the most effective way of using it. There is a charity for children with liver disease – the Michael McGough Foundation – and a great deal of money raised by the *Express* when they covered the story of Gemma Knight has gone to them. There are many individual cases of children who are ill who need help to find cures for their illnesses. The main question is whether to give it away in a series of small sums, or spend it in larger lumps, to try and help more children.

Today I take Catherine to Addenbrooke's. They are desperately short of intensive care equipment there. Catherine meets staff there who start to give her their calculations as to what they need, and how much it will cost. She pops in to see Matthew Whittaker and says he looks very well indeed.

136

Sunday 18th March

Ben goes home for the weekend – another great step forward. He finds a cat in the garden, shouts with laughter and tries to chase it. He finds all his old toys and plays with them – he's up practically all night.

Monday 2nd April

Julie Fewkes goes to Addenbrooke's to see Ben – the first time since he left intensive care. We film her playing with him – as she looks at him her face softens, the tension goes – she looks quite beautiful. Ben walks hand-in-hand between Debbie and Julie – the two women who have given him this chance of life.

Tuesday 10th April

Catherine has put forward her recommendations for the fund. A new fully equipped, fully staffed intensive care room, the Ben Hardwick Room, at Addenbrooke's. And a new medical post, a paediatric fellowship, to work both at King's and Addenbrooke's, treating children with liver disease, and those who need transplants, before and after their operations. She has costed it most carefully. Copies of her proposal go to the Health Authority, the Minister for Health, the doctors and surgeons we have consulted, and we tell the Hardwicks what we've suggested.

Saturday 14th April

Ben is being discharged from hospital this afternoon. The hospital told us at the beginning of the week it might be possible, but then Ben kept running slight temperatures. Still, we arrange to film Professor Calne examining him – he did promise, all those weeks ago, that he would talk to us on film, the day he discharged Ben from hospital. I wonder if any of us really believed that day would ever come. Well, today has arrived, and Ben seems much better. Debbie is there with him, delighted of course, but, as always, aware it can still all go wrong. She's lived with too many set-backs, too much sudden bad news, ever to relax. 'They may have said we can go today,' she tells us, 'But we've still got to run out of that door, yet.'

Professor Calne arrives in his white coat, sits on the bed with Ben, and examines him. Then he looks up at Debbie. 'He's in very good shape,' he says. 'The test results are improving. I'm cautiously pleased.' 'What does that mean?' Esther asks. 'Well,' he says, 'I'm pleased, but I'm cautious.'

We are all very aware that the publicity we have brought must have added a great burden to Professor Calne's already difficult work. What we went through, when we knew a massive transplant operation was being planned, was anxiety enough. How much worse for him. 'We can't have made it easier for you to operate on Ben,' Esther says. 'It was very worrying,' he admits. 'It's always worrying to operate on a child, to operate on anybody, but particularly when it's a child. In this case, since there was a focus of public interest, it was not just Ben, but other children and other people waiting for transplants who were depending on a good result on Ben. And this did make it a little bit worrying . . . a bit more worrying than it otherwise would be. I think this case has been an important one for organ donation. Not just for our work but for the work of others doing transplantation.'

Ben sits on the bed, perfectly happily, as Debbie cuddles him. Esther says, 'It's odd, isn't it, how much one two-year-old boy, who knows nothing about it, can contribute?' Professor Calne says, 'I think it's better that he doesn't know anything about it. Otherwise he might be worried, too!'

The interview ends. Esther walks down the corridor. There, in the room next door, are the other Hardwicks – Andrew's parents. The tests on Andrew are complete now, he is ready and waiting for a transplant. From now on, as the days tick by, he will become less strong, less able to take the onslaught of a huge operation. Ron Hardwick, Andrew's father, looks at Esther with a plea she can't ignore. 'Can you do for Andrew, what you've done for Ben?' he asks. She would love just to say, 'Yes, of course.' But the BBC bosses are getting restless with the continued coverage, anxious for the programme to move on. 'I don't know if we can,' she says. 'But I will interview you now. And I give you my word the interview will be broadcast. If we can't use it on *That's Life*, don't worry, it will still be broadcast.'

They film Andrew, playing. They film his father's desperate plea, to doctors, to bereaved parents, to remember that they could save his dying son.

On our way out of hospital, we call in to see Matthew Whittaker. It is clear he has been terribly ill. In fact he very nearly died. He has tubes all over his body – and posters all over his room – 'This Way to Matthew's Cocktail Bar.' His parents have engaged in a desperate fight to keep his indomitable will to live going. They joke, and laugh, and Matthew, underneath all those tubes, manages a smile. He is determined to survive.

We pay a quick visit to the main transplant ward; a row of people who owe their lives to that merciful decision, to say yes to organ donation. It is usually the young who favour donation, it is usually the young, their lives tragically cut short by accident or sudden illness, who become donors. Old people fear it as an idea sometimes, but usually it's an unrealistic fear. Few old people are suitable as donors.

When we return to London, Esther goes straight to Gordon. 'Is there any way we can show this interview?' Without hesitation, Gordon says, 'We must. It's our responsibility. You can't be in a position of perhaps being able to save a little boy like that, and then not do everything possible. We will certainly run the interview.' Not for the last time, Esther is grateful for the good sense and compassion Gordon invariably shows at moments like this.

They show the film in the programme. Two weeks later, Andrew has his transplant, and it's a success.

Sunday 15th April

Ben appears on the programme, just at the end, while we are wishing our viewers a happy Easter. Life out of death, the theme of Easter. Esther hands Ben a silver balloon – he is enchanted with it. The audience is enchanted with him. The red lights go out, the programme is finished – Ben sits on a stool and recites 'Baa Baa Black Sheep' to a spellbound studio audience. Esther swears mildly. If only he'd done that on the programme. Never mind – he has achieved enough, this little boy.

CHAPTER FOURTEEN

As spring becomes summer, Ben grows stronger. Our researches into the best way to use the Ben Hardwick fund are completed. We carefully cost the new intensive care room, with equipment and staff at Addenbrooke's Hospital. Many viewers have suggested that the new doctor's teaching post should be named after Matthew Fewkes – and Debbie Hardwick and Julie Fewkes are both delighted. To celebrate the last programme of the series, in July we decide to film some of the children again. When the pictures of Ben arrive back in the cutting room, Esther catches her breath. He is playing games with his mother and father, the sunlight on his hair, in a summer meadow full of buttercups. Esther's dream, that no one had thought possible, is there, in the sunlight.

Nothing is perfect, nothing is for ever. However long these transplant children live, they will be taking special drugs to combat rejection, and they face the risk of liver failure. But every new month is a month of life they have gained – and the parents who breathe each new day with them look on transplant surgery as a true miracle. It is a miracle created by the compassion of the donor family, the skill and dedication of the medical team, the generosity of the people who give money to fund it, and the courage of the children. In our last programme of the series, we try to bring these themes together:

ESTHER: It is really extraordinary to know that last January, in the second programme of this series, we told you then that Ben was not expected to live more than a few weeks. But then, of course, Mr and Mrs Fewkes came forward when their own baby, Matthew, tragically died and allowed him to become a donor for the first liver transplant on a baby as young as Ben. Well, this week, Gavin went down to meet Ben with his father and mother in the fields by the river near their home. Gavin asked Debbie to look back over the last six months.

(Film)

DEBBIE: Every emotion that you could possibly feel we have felt in the last six months. We feel we owe so many people so much. But also, there was obviously the sorrow and the anxiety. And yet, if things went wrong tomorrow for Ben, it would still have been worth it. The last six months would still have been worth it, because we've got something now that we never had before. We've had hope. The last six months, we've had a child that possibly could go to school one day, that could come out here today, and play by the river. Six months ago, that wasn't possible. Now, maybe, he can go to school. Maybe, he can be a normal child. At least, we've had that hope. We've had something.

GAVIN: Debbie, d'you think Ben's given hope to other children with this liver disease?

DEBBIE: Well, I think it's lovely now that no other mother has actually got to go through what I went through, and what lots of other people have been through before me. Living for two years with a child that is dying, and being told, time and time again, that there is nothing that can be done for him. Looking for a cure, looking for something, and coming up against brick wall after brick wall. Nobody now has got to face that.

(Film ends)

ESTHER: And, of course, it is not just children with Ben's liver disease who now have fresh hope. There have been more transplants of all kinds, since Ben's story. Kidney transplants, for example, have gone up 40 per cent in the last six months. John Patten is the Parliamentary Under-Secretary for Health. He told us:

BILL: 'I would like to say a very warm thank you to *That's Life* for the way it has brought home to so many people the unique life-saving value of transplantation, and the way in which the

141

tragedy of an early death can mean the gift of life for someone else. The courage of those involved in the Ben Hardwick story must have been an inspiration to very many people. I hope that this will be remembered, and that more and more people will carry a donor card and make it a shared family decision.'

ESTHER: Well, it is very kind of him to say we played a part. But, of course, by far the greatest part was played by all those viewers who were moved by the story and wanted to help. In fact, with projects all up and down the country, you have raised so much money that we are now able to equip the Ben Hardwick Room in Addenbrooke's Hospital, Cambridge, the intensive-care room they so desperately need for very ill children. Professor Calne, who operated on Ben, told us:

MICHAEL: 'In the past, we have sometimes been unable to perform transplants because there was no bed available. This room is going to make an enormous difference to us.'

ESTHER: We are also going to use some of the money to set up a special doctor's post to look after children with liver disease. A great many of you felt that it should be named after Matthew Fewkes, the little boy who tragically died and whose parents, Julie and Darryl Fewkes, allowed his liver to be donated to Ben. Julie is with us tonight and so we can show you, Julie, the advertisement that appears in the *British Medical Journal* for the Matthew Fewkes Fellowship in Paediatrics. And, in addition, we have made a donation to the hospital where Matthew was treated: the Queen's Medical Centre, in Nottingham, to buy toys and equipment for the children's ward where Matthew spent so much time.

Now, what about some of the other children we've told you about during the series, those who would have died without a liver transplant?

BILL: Andrew Hardwick, not related to Ben but with the same illness, we told you last February was desperately ill and getting weaker. In April, he went to Addenbrooke's in the hope that a transplant might be possible and it was. On the first of May, he had his operation.

ESTHER: So, this week Gavin went to meet Andrew and talk to his father, Ron Hardwick, and they looked back to those darkest moments when they had no idea there could be hope for their baby because there were no donors for babies like Andrew.

(Film)

RON: The worst period was Christmas of last year. I think when he was becoming a person, growing up, two years old – that was the time when we were playing with his Christmas toys and there were tears of sadness. You can't explain how you feel when you're looking at him on Christmas Day, and his toys are here, and you daren't think about next Christmas, you daren't think about next week. They were tears of sadness, but they're tears of joy now. It seems as though he was on loan to us before. Everybody was telling us he wasn't going to live, and we wanted to cram so much of his days in, and every day we had was a bonus. Now, he's just there. He's very well. He's enjoying his life, and we're enjoying his life.

(Film ends)

ESTHER: Well, he certainly looks a picture of health now. Perhaps you also remember Matthew Whittaker. He is eleven, he had his liver transplant last March and when we showed him first, he looked quite delicate. Well, he's with us here tonight and you look marvellous, Matthew. What Matthew doesn't know is what Professor Calne, his surgeon, said about him. He says you have been very brave indeed. You had a very difficult time after the operation but, even in your worst weeks, you stayed cheerful and kept joking and he thinks you deserve a medal for bravery. That's what Professor Calne says. *(Applause)* And I'm sure we all feel that round of applause goes for Matthew's parents too. And we would like to pass on our own medals for bravery to those other anonymous people – all over the country – the families of donors who have allowed transplants to happen and allowed so many lives to be saved.

The sight of children like Ben and Andrew and Matthew must make them feel how worthwhile it is. So, with that thought, I'm afraid we must leave you.

We hope you all have a lovely summer. We will be back with you in January. Until then, from us all, goodnight.

November 1984

Professor Calne holds a Christmas party at Addenbrooke's for the liver transplant children, and all the other transplant patients. Andrew Hardwick is there, craftily sneaking extra slices of his father's cake. Ron looks at him, and laughs. 'Our friends say Andrew takes his medicine and we get better,' he says, face alight with happiness. 'This time last year we were celebrating his birthday six months early, because we didn't think he'd be alive to see it. Now every day's a birthday.'

A little girl, slender and delicate as a fairy doll, sits next to Professor Calne. He explains her story to us. 'Christine Brock had a transplant, and some days later she suddenly went into liver failure. In another six hours she would have been dead. At that moment a donor came forward, and we were able to perform another transplant. If the donor had come forward the day before, we would not have taken the liver – we wouldn't have known it was necessary. One day later would have been too late.' Christine grins up at him, untouched by the close embrace she's had with death. She is so alive now, as she smiles cheekily up at Professor Calne, and calls him 'a typical man'. But she's not a 'typical child'. With two liver transplants behind her, Christine now works and plays, runs and dances like any other child.

Transplant operations will continue, as long as donors make them possible. Some of them will fail, some lives will be lost. But as we stand in that special party in Addenbrooke's Hospital, watching the happiness of the children who have been saved, and the joy of their parents who have been given hope, their joy is infectious. Ben is there with his mother and father, Debbie and Billy, who are living separately now, but united in their battle for the little boy they both adore. 'I can't say thank you,' Debbie says, 'to the people who have given a child the gift of life. No parent can ever thank them enough.'

Perhaps, seeing the children themselves is thanks enough.

CHAPTER FIFTEEN

The new series begins in January 1985. Each year we start again with trepidation, wondering whether we'll be welcomed back as friends into our viewers' sitting rooms, or if this time they'll groan at the thought of us, and firmly switch us off. In fact, to our delight and astonishment they switch us on in greater numbers – we reach eighteen million viewers. It's as if we have come of age, grown up, gained understanding and concern. Maybe the story of Ben has taught us how to be more effective as programme-makers.

We have filmed the Christmas party at Addenbrooke's hospital, and include a particularly moving interview with Professor Calne and Christine Brock, the little girl who has had two liver transplants: Professor Calne explains what a miracle it was that a donor came forward when Christine's first transplant had just failed; in another six hours she would have died. 'It couldn't have come at a more exact, perfect time to be of value to her,' he tells Esther. 'I think that more and more often this kind of emergency liver transplant may become necessary, as there are more patients being transplanted.'

John Morrell, our new programme editor, watches the film of the party. Ben is sitting on his father's lap playing with a balloon, his mother watching him proudly, while Matthew Whittaker cuts the Christmas cake, and Andrew Hardwick runs round like the boisterous, healthy three-year-old he now is. He plans to broadcast it in our programme at the end of January, to mark the anniversary of Ben's transplant. The Fewkes are about to have another baby – so we decide to send Julie and Darryl our best wishes too. And we have also had a letter from a consultant at the children's kidney unit at Guy's Hospital. She says:

Last year we nearly doubled our kidney transplants – from 27 to 46 children. We were all, patients, family and staff, very grateful. But now we have 30 children urgently needing new kidneys and we have only had one kidney donated in the past month. Could you possibly remind Britain that they are so badly needed?

On Saturday, the day before the programme, Shaun goes to Guy's Hospital, with our photographer Les Wilson, to see some of these children. The picture of the ward of children engraves itself on Shaun's memory – children who have to spend whole days hooked up to dialysis machines. Samantha, a serious little twelve-year-old girl, carefully attaches herself to the needle and tubes, and explains to Shaun what the machine does. Her blood system has to pass through the machine which, in effect replaces her kidneys, by doing the work her own kidneys should perform for her, but no longer can. Like all the children, these machines are saving her life, but it is a harrowing process. With a transplant she could become a normal child, leading an ordinary life, released from this ordeal. No wonder their consultant wrote to us in desperation.

Les takes pictures of a dozen children, and we show them in our programme. But Esther and Shaun are becoming anxious. How long must we continue to make programmes to 'remind Britain' in the doctor's words, how desperately transplants are needed? Our MORI opinion poll had shown that 77 per cent of people are prepared to become donors. 71 per cent are actually in favour of an opt-out system, where most people would be regarded as potential donors, unless they have registered an objection. How else will willing donors ever be matched with the patients who urgently need transplants? Must we really broadcast an appeal like this every month?

Three weeks later we are reminded again of the defects in the present system. On Sunday 10th February, while we are preparing the programme, Addenbrooke's rings Esther's home. Desmond immediately tells them to contact the studio. They are fighting for the life of a baby in acute liver failure. Would we have time in tonight's programme to broadcast an appeal? If any hospital staff in intensive care are working with a possible donor family, could they please ask the relatives if they would agree to a transplant? By chance, in this programme we are dealing with the subject of unsafe riding hats, and the tragic death of a fourteen-year-old girl, Kerry Ayliffe. She had been a skilful rider, she had worn her riding hat correctly, but it had failed to protect her skull, and when she fell from her pony, she suffered fatal brain injury. Her family had written to us to warn other riders, but her mother put a postscript to her letter:

As a footnote, we would like to thank you for your publicity on transplants. Because of your programme, we discussed the subject as a family and when we were told that Kerry was dying, we knew that she would want to help others. Her kidneys were both used successfully in transplants and it is some small comfort to know that two other young people have been given a future.

The call from Addenbrooke's reaches us just in time to include the appeal in the programme. But this time Esther has very little hope. 'The baby will die in a matter of hours,' she says to Shaun. 'How can we find a donor, and save her? The people we are trying to reach will never be watching television tonight, they will be working in intensive care units in hospitals round the country. It's dreadful that Addenbrooke's have to ring us in this emergency.' Shaun agrees. 'They have contacted every hospital in their area,' he says. 'But obviously that's not enough. They should be able to pass an urgent message to every hospital. Why doesn't UK Transplant have a computer terminal with a screen in every intensive care unit, so they can give details of real emergencies, like this one?' We broadcast the appeal, but it is, as we had feared, too late. The baby dies.

Over the next few weeks, other stories absorb us. It is a terrible winter, the coldest for many years, and among our letters there are many from families – the very old and the very young being most at risk – imprisoned in damp, freezing houses. Some of the homes are Victorian, their bricks crumbling and unable to keep out the driving rain and sleet. Some, even more shockingly, are quite modern, just badly designed and built. Les Wilson travels round the country building up a photographic dossier of walls wringing wet with condensation, and smeared with black mould. Catherine

Boyd, her work on the Ben Hardwick Appeal Fund completed, goes to meet the families imprisoned in their council-built slums. For the first time in more than a year, we lose touch with Ben. We haven't spoken to Debbie for almost a month. So when at the end of March tragedy strikes the Hardwick family, and us with them, we are completely unprepared for it.

SHAUN'S DIARY

Saturday 23rd March

I arrive in Cambridge with my parents. It's a special day, not least because I see my family so rarely – as my mother points out to me from time to time, television seems to devour the lives of the people who work on it. As we drive into Cambridge I glance at the billboard of the *Cambridge Evening News*. In block capitals, black on white, it reads LIVER BABY BEN DIES. For a minute I simply can't take it in, can't speak. Can it be our Ben? I know it must be. My parents haven't seen it. I tell them and we drive on in silence.

As we arrive at my old college, the head porter, Mr Griffiths, rushes out with a message. Will I ring Esther straightaway. 'I'm very sorry,' he says. Clearly he has heard the news. 'Please use my office.'

I ring Esther. She has just been telephoned by the Cambridge newspaper. We ask each other questions, stupidly, neither of us knowing the answers. What has gone wrong? Ben had seemed so happy at the Christmas party, we'd not heard that he'd been unwell since, there'd been no warning that his life was in danger. I say I will discover what I can while I am in Cambridge, and we agree to meet at Esther's house that evening.

All day the bulletins carry the news of Ben's death. They say he'd had a second liver transplant. People keep coming up to me – old friends from college – saying how sorry they are to hear the news of his death.

At eight o'clock I arrive at Esther's. Bryher Scudamore, our associate producer, and John Morrell, our editor, are already there. We talk through the decisions we will have to make. Clearly we must broadcast a tribute to Ben, and to all the people who had fought to save his life. We will need the details, discover how it

148

happened. I get on the phone to Professor Calne. He sounds tired – understandably since he's been operating on Ben all night. But this tiredness is not just lack of sleep – it's the tremendous sadness, the disappointment. He has wanted so much to save this little boy.

He explains that in the last few weeks Ben had a series of infections which had damaged his liver. It had become clear that he must have a second transplant if he was to survive. On Friday, while he was at Addenbrooke's for a check-up, a donor was found. The liver matched Ben exactly. Professor Calne and Debbie decided to go ahead. They told Billy, who was in London, and he rushed down to Cambridge to join them.

The operation lasted from 10 o'clock that night until 6 in the morning. It was far more difficult than the first transplant. Ben's heart kept stopping; they had to start it again electrically. They finished the operation. Ben was taken out of the theatre, and into intensive care. They made him comfortable in the Ben Hardwick Room.

One hour later, Ben's heart stopped again. This time they could not start it, it was impossible to revive him. At 7 in the morning, Ben died.

I put the phone down. Professor Calne is preparing for another transplant this evening. Having operated all through the previous night, he will operate again until dawn. Not for the first time I marvel at his stamina, and his team's. They all loved Ben. Now they had lost a patient who meant so much to them, and Ben had transformed their work, enabled them to use their skill to save lives. Was all their work in the balance now? A year ago, one cynical medical journal had predicted 'A few well-publicised failures could undermine public confidence and set the programme back years.' Our campaign to save lives might boomerang disastrously, they said, if any of the children died. Now Ben himself was dead. Would that tragic prediction come true, and transplant surgery be halted for lack of donors?

We replay the pictures from some of our past programmes about Ben, preparing a tribute. Esther is particularly moved by the collection of sequences Bob Marsland, our director, first edited together last summer. To the music of Ben's own favourite song, the one he used to dance to, 'Ben' sung by Michael Jackson, Bob has put shots of Ben playing with bubbles, riding the rocking horse in the hospital, chuckling with delight at a cat, and finally running in the sunlight, surrounded with buttercups, his parents beside him. Perhaps that is the best way to remember Ben – not as a hospital patient, but tasting the freedom of any other three-year-old, in that last, happy year.

Esther and I work until 2 in the morning on the script. She leaves space for the comments she asks me to add tomorrow, from Kenneth Clark, the Minister for Health, and from the other parents whose children have been saved by liver transplants. In the early hours I get home to my flat to find my parents there, still waiting up for me. I try to apologise for ruining our day, but of course they understand.

Sunday 24th March

I manage to contact Kenneth Clark, one of the few politicians who speaks clearly and vividly without formal jargon. His statement underlines just how much Ben's story has achieved, while also expressing the great sadness everyone feels about Ben's death. He says 'I'm so sorry to hear this news. The death of a child is always particularly sad, but especially this little chap, who has fought so bravely. Many lives have been saved, because of him. The increase in the number of donors has saved not just children, but adults too. It is very important now that people don't feel discouraged by his death, that families and hospital staff don't become afraid to offer organs to make transplant surgery continue.' Mr Clark ends by asking us to send his sympathy not just to Ben's parents, but to the families of donors whose hopes have been disappointed, and he praises the courage of everyone who has been fighting to save Ben's life.

Matthew Whittaker is one of the children who owe their life-saving transplant to Ben's example. When I ring the Whittakers' home, Matthew himself answers the phone, out of breath from running down stairs. I am struck by his vitality – his mother Irene tells me, 'It's wonderful how well Matthew is now. Ben gave Matthew the chance to live.'

I speak to Celia Wight at Addenbrooke's, and to Andrew Hardwick's father, Ron. Debbie is staying with her parents.

150

Knowing how she must be feeling, I ring her, as much to express how much she and her family are in our thoughts, as to ask her for any information. She sounds numb, as if the pain has not really begun to hit her. Then suddenly she says, 'He did go to school, you know. That was always my dream, that one day he could go to school like any other little boy, and he did. Just before the operation he spent a morning there, I remember how he took his little black plimsolls with him.' The poignancy of the everyday detail lacerates her, and nearly brings us both to tears.

When I reach the television theatre, it seems to be in even greater chaos than normal. Eighty-two drum majorettes have arrived, to sing an appeal for rehearsal rooms big enough for them all. They certainly do need a good deal of space – and as they parade up and down the stage, two BBC firemen in uniform watch, shaking their heads. 'Can't be done,' I hear one of them say. 'Insufficient dressing rooms for eighty-two, against the rules to allow this in the programme. Sorry, you'll have to stop all this, regulations are regulations.' Clearly there will have to be protracted negotiations if this item is to go ahead at all – in the end the negotiations are so protracted they take up nearly all our rehearsal time. So we never really have a chance to rehearse the Ben item we have put together, to see if it strikes the right note.

Letters are already arriving at the stage door, some of them containing money, all of them sending sympathy to the Hardwick family. Esther and John Morrell decide to open the programme by thanking all the viewers for their response and for positively demonstrating their compassion and generosity. The last adjustments to the script are made – miraculously the chaos becomes order at the very last moment, and the programme begins. The drum majorettes have found a loophole in BBC regulations and march, trumpets blaring and batons twirling, all over the stage. We report on the fact that some big stores, as a result of one of our other campaigns, have now decided to sell children's pyjamas that have been made flame-resistant. There is a charming film about a dog who acts as a bartender in a pub in Devon. And then, as we near the end of the programme, I see Esther dig her nails hard into the palms of her hands. We come to our tribute to Ben.

151

ESTHER: Perhaps you remember, exactly a year ago, it was just before Easter, a little boy was carried into this studio here. Ben Hardwick had just come out of hospital after his liver transplant. (*Film pictures*) He was very happy that day. Do you remember how he loved the silver balloon we gave him? Well, a year later, after another transplant operation, Ben has just died.

But the first thing we must say to you is that Ben's last year was very happy. He recovered so quickly from that major operation he was almost at once playing with a bicycle in the hospital play-room, or with his favourite bubbles, or laughing with the nurses. And then, taking his first steps.

Three months after the operation, he left hospital and, of course, he was very happy to be back at home with his parents. In the summer, he even played on the beach, which was something he had never been allowed to do before, and one of our viewers arranged for the whole family to go to Malta for two weeks.

We last saw Ben at Christmas, at the party the hospital gave all the children who had had liver transplants and, once again, he was very happy.

So, yesterday, we spoke to his surgeon, Professor Roy Calne and asked him what went wrong. He said:

GAVIN: 'When we first performed the transplant a year ago, Ben was very well. In fact, we were amazed how quickly he pulled through. After all, we had had to wait so long to operate because, at that time, there were no donors, that we thought it was already too late. His liver had deteriorated so badly that by the time Debbie, his mother, had contacted you, and a donor was found, he had only a few weeks to live. It is impossible to say how pleased we were that he could be saved and it was Ben's determination and courage then that pulled him through. It was only five or six months after the operation that we realised the liver we had given him was not the best match.'

ESTHER: Did you consider a second transplant then?

GAVIN: 'We considered it, but not urgently. We weren't

152

worried because he seemed so happy and he was such a bright, lively little chap.'

ESTHER: In fact, I remember spending a day at the zoo with him in the summer. He was obviously enjoying life.

GAVIN: 'Yes, but in the last few months, he has been getting infections which have progressively damaged his liver. It still wasn't serious until a few weeks ago. In the past two weeks, he became so ill his only chance was another liver transplant. On Friday, a liver became available and, this time, it was a perfect match for Ben.'

ESTHER: Which means another child must have died and that child's family must have agreed to let him become a donor?

GAVIN: 'Yes. Only since Ben have families come forward like this to make liver transplants on children possible. Debbie decided with us that the transplant should go ahead. We started at 10 o'clock on Friday. Things did not go well. Throughout the operation, his heart kept stopping but we knew from the way he had fought so bravely before that if anybody had a chance he did. But one hour after the operation, he died.'

ESTHER: Was all your effort wasted then – the two operations wasted?

GAVIN: 'Certainly not. I wish we could have saved Ben. He has saved so many other people – adults and children, who would have died if it had not been for him. Twelve children who have had liver transplants since his first transplant are alive now who would otherwise be dead.'

ESTHER: In fact, without Ben, there would not have been a single liver transplant on children in this country because there were no child-donors. Doctors simply could not ask bereaved families so families never knew that this was a way to save another life.

Celia Wight is the Transplant Co-ordinator at Addenbrooke's Hospital in Cambridge. She told us today:

BILL: 'Ben was a gorgeous child – everyone in the hospital loved him. We got to know him well over the last year and it's almost impossible to believe the change he seems to have made in transplant surgery in this country – not just liver transplants, the number of kidney transplants, and heart transplants have doubled and there have been ten times the number of corneal transplants which have meant that people can see again.'

ESTHER: This morning, we talked to two families who have very good reason to be grateful to Ben. Firstly, do you remember Matthew Whittaker? He was the first child to have a liver transplant after Ben and his mother told us:

GAVIN: 'Matthew was beginning to lose his will to live before Ben's story was told. There didn't seem to be much hope. Ben changed everything. He gave Matthew the chance to live. It is wonderful how well he is now.'

ESTHER: Another little boy called Andrew Hardwick also had a liver transplant, thanks to Ben. His father, Ron, told us:

BILL: 'It was a terrible shock to hear about Ben. It is heart-breaking, because – but for Ben – Andrew wouldn't be here today. They knew each other well, they had a special friendship which was very moving. Andrew will miss him terribly. I can't put into words what we feel for Ben and his family today.'

ESTHER: And also this morning, we spoke to Kenneth Clark, the Minister for Health. He told us:

GAVIN: 'I am so sorry to hear this news. The death of a child is always particularly sad but especially this little chap who had fought so bravely. Many lives have been saved because of him. The increase in the number of donors has saved not just children but adults too. It is very important now that people don't feel discouraged by his death, that families and hospital staff don't become afraid to offer organs to make transplant surgery continue. When Ben had his transplant a year ago, he helped people realise that, even in tragedy, the death of a child can allow another child to be given the chance to live. I hope very much that people in the future won't hesitate to offer help to other children like him. My thoughts are very much with Mr and Mrs Hardwick and I would like to send my sympathy to all his family and also to the families of the donors whose hopes have been disappointed, but also I would like to congratulate his

154

parents for the courage they have shown in their fight to save his life.'

ESTHER: In addition to the attitudes that Ben has changed, the money that was raised by the Ben Hardwick Transplant Appeal Fund has furnished and staffed this intensive care room and paid for a doctor to work for children with serious liver disease in the Matthew Fewkes Fellowship. These aren't bad achievements for one little three-year-old boy. But has the fight, the worry, the whole ordeal been worth it for his family?

We hope they realise how much good they have done, how many lives they have saved. We know they never had false hope, they always knew Ben's life was precarious. Last summer, the Hardwicks took their little boy out into the sunshine and Debbie told us how she felt.

(Film)

DEBBIE: If things went wrong tomorrow for Ben, it would still have been worth it. The last six months would still have been worth it because we've got something now that we never had before. We've had hope. The last six months, we've had a child that possibly could go to school and could come out here today and play by the river and everything. Six months ago, that wasn't possible.

ESTHER: Well, Ben did go to school. And he gave his parents a great deal of joy in those last few months. And so we send our sympathy to all the people who loved Ben and have cared for him and we ask them to remember the good he has done, in his three years.

We have to say good night to you now but may we just leave you with the pictures of Ben's last year – his last happy year – the year that no one expected him to have – with the song that was Ben's own favourite song. It's called 'Ben'.

(Film ends)

The music of Ben's favourite song fills the studio, as the pictures blend into each other – Ben smiling, Ben laughing, his huge eyes shining with happiness. And then that final scene, in the field of buttercups. He looks up and points to the sun – the pictures stop

155

and hold that moment, and the programme ends. We have decided to remove our jolly signature tune, the list of credits we normally run – how can you follow that last perfect image of a child in the sun, who has come to mean so much to us all?

There is complete silence in the studio audience. It seems to last for minutes on end. Not a cough, not a whisper – as if we are all under a spell. The studio crew stand like statues. I've never known a moment like this, in the silence we are all paying our own tribute to Ben, and to everyone involved in loving him, and fighting for him. Above all there is a feeling of unbearable sadness – we have tried to emphasise positive comfort, the happiness of the last year. But nobody in the studio can believe that Ben has gone now, for ever.

Esther breaks the silence. Two ladies have come to the studio with a cheque for the Ben Hardwick Fund – their visit was planned weeks ago – so that they can hand the money over to Esther immediately after the programme. She calls them up onto the stage. As they give her the cheque, it is clear that they have been crying – their eyes are still brimming with tears. Esther tries to comfort them. 'Perhaps with this money we can start a new fund in Ben's name, the Ben Hardwick Memorial Fund. If we can continue to save children's lives, what better way to preserve Ben's memory?' We all meet after the programme, not really knowing if it has gone well or not. But Esther and I are quite clear in our own minds that a Ben Hardwick Memorial Fund could be created, should be created, as soon as possible.

CHAPTER SIXTEEN

Esther arrives home at almost midnight on Sunday to find a message waiting for her. 'Please ring Debbie.' She goes straight to her desk, and dials the number. They talk for a long time. Debbie has seen the programme, of course, and is very moved. She tells Esther all the stages of this last terrible weekend – the moment on Friday when she was told a donor had come forward, the discussions with Professor Calne, the wild painful scenes with Billy when he hears that Ben has died. 'I've been thinking about Julie Fewkes so much during the last two days,' Debbie says. 'I think I know what she must be feeling – and that she will understand the way I feel, now.' Julie has moved house in Nottingham, so Esther promises to try and find her new phone number and put the two families in touch with each other. Both, now, are mourning Ben. Esther mentions the idea of a new fund, in Ben's memory. 'I would like to help,' Debbie says, 'I would very much like to be involved with any new work to save other children.' Esther agrees – Debbie obviously must be closely involved. Debbie talks about the very end of this evening's programme, the haunting Michael Jackson song, 'Ben', accompanying pictures of her little boy at his most beautiful. 'He was so well, in that last year, so well,' Debbie says. Esther puts the phone down at the end of their conversation, a little heartened. At least Debbie has been supported and comforted by the programme.

The next day Esther and a film team catch the breakfast plane to Glasgow to film some street interviews. At the sight of the camera, crowds collect which make it impossible for them to continue. People take Esther's hand, asking her to pass on to the Hardwicks and the Fewkes their sympathy and good wishes. One man tells her in anger that a local paper has carried an article attacking the transplant programme, describing it as a costly series of experiments doomed to failure. Could this be the start of a back-lash? With the memory of all those other lives saved and enhanced by transplantation, Esther hopes that this would turn out to be one eccentric article, not the start of a destructive campaign against transplants.

She returns to London that evening to find that Julie Fewkes is in London, too, so Esther rings her and passes on Debbie's message. Julie says 'Of course I have been thinking of her, too. If I can be any help at all, I'd love to talk to her. I would like to come to Ben's funeral, if that's all right.' Esther puts Julie and Debbie in touch with each other. No doubt they have thoughts and feelings which no outsider can share.

On the day of the funeral, Shaun and Esther arrive at Debbie's parents' house. Outside, the flowers are being collected, including a golden teddy bear lovingly constructed out of spring flowers, sunshine yellow. Inside the house, they meet Professor Calne's wife. He himself couldn't come to the funeral, for the best of all reasons. Since Ben's operation, so many donors have been found that he has been able to perform three more liver transplants, and six kidney transplants. He has been operating round the clock. He is still operating. Mrs Calne is very encouraging; she believes that there will not be a backlash. 'How can you be unmoved when you see children like Christine Brock and Andrew Hardwick who would not be walking around now, but for Ben.'

Celia Wight is there, and Odette Charmant, the nurse in charge of the transplant unit. It is very poignant to see how many senior members of Addenbrooke's Hospital staff have made the journey to come to Ben's funeral. Debbie herself is still locked in the numb calmness that surrounds her at moments of greatest anxiety and sorrow, and gave her the strength to fight for her son's life. Now that fight is over, but she needs the strength today more than ever before. It is the day she most dreaded, the day all of us had fearfully anticipated so often. We set off for the church.

There are quiet crowds outside; the only noise is the snap of photographers' cameras. 'They asked me if I wanted a private funeral,' Debbie has told Esther, 'but I said no. So many people loved Ben I felt they had a right to be there.' In fact BBC Television news put together a careful thoughtful tribute to Ben in their bulletin that night, with interviews from other parents desperately hoping for life-saving transplants for their children.

The small white coffin at the front of the church seems peaceful, at rest. The congregation sing 'The Lord is my shepherd', and 'Morning has broken'. The vicar speaks of 'Little Ben, whose fight has helped save so many other lives and so perhaps we should think of him not as little Ben but as Big Ben.' And he quotes from a viewer's letter: 'When he smiled he really did make the whole nation smile with him.' As we leave the church, a woman seizes Esther's hand. 'I must thank you for telling Ben's story,' she says. 'It has done so much good, I just felt I had to thank you, all of you.' Then she disappears back into the crowd. The reporters gather round Esther. 'Have you a comment for us?' 'I can only think about the lovely little boy I knew,' she says, inadequately. And then, 'But also about the other people, children and adults, who are alive now because of him. Professor Calne himself has performed nine transplant operations in the last three days. Ben is still saving lives.'

The cremation ceremony is more painful. Outside the chapel stands a tiny snooker table made of flowers, from Billy and his family, to mark Ben's favourite game. Billy stands beside it, unseeing, his eyes streaming with tears. The rest of us long to be able to comfort him, but we hold back, knowing at this moment he is inconsolable.

After the cremation, Shaun and Esther join the Hardwick family. Julie Fewkes is there with her daughter Vicky, and her new baby, Samantha. As Julie gazes at Samantha, bonny and smiling in her pram, Esther sees in her face the softness, the tenderness, she'd shown the day she first played with Ben. 'Would it have been easier for you, Julie,' Esther asks, 'if you had never known that Matthew's liver was being used to save Ben? Would you rather you had helped an anonymous child, and that your own identity had never been revealed?' Julie nods. 'The publicity has been terrible,' she says. 'And now I feel as if I've lost another child.' Irene Whittaker is sitting next to Julie – she has brought both her sons to the funeral, to pay tribute to the little boy who has helped to give Matthew Whittaker the gift of life. 'It's been much easier for me,' Irene says, 'never knowing which child was the donor for Matthew's operation. I never had to go through the personal tragedy of the donor family's bereavement. Although of course my gratitude to them is immeasurable. It's far easier for me not knowing who they are.'

Esther digests the lesson. Although *That's Life* had not been responsible for tracking down and exposing the identity of the Fewkes family, when the first press conference was held, Esther had been there with the rest of the press to meet them. And as a result, Matthew himself now has his own memorial, in the doctor's post dedicated to him, and in the donations to Nottingham Hospital in his name. But the price for the Fewkes was the pain of all the publicity, and now the second bereavement. Subsequent donors have usually had their anonymity preserved. Perhaps it is easier that way, in the long run.

When Esther and Shaun get back to the *That's Life* office, they find hundreds more letters. One lady from Wales writes:

'My husband and I would be most grateful if you, on your programme, would thank the parents of the donor who gave my husband the chance to live, with a heart transplant. Eddie is really fit and well now. We both shared the heartbreak and the joy when Ben was given a liver transplant, and I feel sure the programme helped many people to have a second chance to live, like my husband. We have never met the donor's parents, but may we thank them from the bottom of our hearts. To make such a decision at a time of trouble is a brave act indeed.

Then we read a letter from another viewer with a special reason to be grateful to Ben. She is a nurse in Portsmouth, and she says:

We were saddened to hear of Ben Hardwick's death. I have good reason to be grateful to that lovely little lad, as in June 1984 I underwent a heart transplant at Harefield Hospital. There is no doubt that the story of Ben went a long way to make the public aware of the need for donor organs. I agree with you that we should look positively at the extra life Ben was given. Like many other transplant patients I am grateful for every extra day I have been given. The gift of life is a wonderful thing, and thanks to the unselfish bravery of someone and his family I am able to enjoy life to the full. If I should die tomorrow, it will all have been worthwhile, every wonderful moment of it. Please continue your much needed work in making the public aware of the need for donor organs and the fact that transplant surgery does work. I, like the majority of heart transplant patients, live a fit, healthy and normal life. I run a house, and I have returned part-time to my former job as a nurse on the coronary-care unit of my local hospital.

Then a letter arrives from Mrs Stanley (the liver transplant patient who first wrote to us a year ago, offering hope to Debbie, and whose letter Esther had read to Debbie before that first operation on Ben). Mrs Stanley says now:

I wrote to you at the beginning of little Ben's story, and I was so pleased he was admitted the following day, and safely underwent a liver transplant. It is now with very great sadness that I write again, having just heard of Ben's death. So much has been done by so many to try and save that dear little boy. I am glad I had the opportunity myself to visit him and play with him, and I was touched by his cheerfulness and friendliness to everyone, considering his age and what he had been through. He gave me a big smile and blew me a kiss, when I last saw him.

I wish to pay great tribute to your programme, you have done so much to help the transplant programme to move forward, and it is some consolation to know Ben hasn't died in vain.

I am sure I speak for millions when I extend my sympathy to Debbie and Billy Hardwick, and all their family, in the tragic loss of their little boy, and a special thought for Mr and Mrs Fewkes, too. Ben is at peace now, together with Matthew Fewkes, may God bless everyone for all the help they gave.

Hundreds of letters reach us from other parents who identify with Debbie and Billy, and ask us to pass on their sympathy, and the love they too felt for Ben. One mother says:

I felt I must write to you. If possible, please pass my thoughts and prayers to Debbie. I have two sons of my own, and when I saw your programme and heard Debbie first appealing for help, like many other people I took Ben into my heart. I will find it difficult to forget his sweet face. As the day has passed I have begun to think about Debbie, it is going to be so difficult for her, after spending these last three years devoting her life to Ben. She has been a marvellous mother, hasn't she? So maybe you could pass on my thoughts to her – I shall be thinking of her.

Shaun sits lost for words after reading another letter, from a bereaved mother. She writes to Debbie and Billy:

Just a few words to say how sorry I was to hear that 'our Ben' had died. Last September my own son died in a car accident, so I do know a little of what you feel like.

All I can say really is that if my Mark brought people half the happiness in his eighteen years that Ben did in his three, then I shall be happy. Mark himself was keenly interested in Ben's progress, and would be sad for you.

There are many letters from children. Jill, aged 11, writes to Debbie and Billy:

When I saw *That's Life* last night, I went upstairs and cried. I do really feel sorry for you both, I think you are both very brave, and if Ben had lived he would have had the best mum and dad ever. Sorry the letter is so short, but I have to go to school.

Barry, who's 10, says:

I really am very sorry about what happened to Ben. I was very upset when I heard about him on the news. I was one of Ben's best fans and I used to have a fight with my mum to watch *That's Life* when I first heard about him. Ben was a very brave boy and I'll never forget him – I really am sorry. Ben deserves to be remembered.

Ben *will* be remembered. In the two weeks after his death, Shaun meets again the anonymous donor who backed the first fund set up in Ben's name. Together they formalise the arrangements for a new charity fund, the Ben Hardwick Memorial Fund. The purpose of the charity will be to provide donations to any established unit devoted to saving children's lives, which is now under financial threat. These days, when public money is so short, children have sometimes to be turned away from hospital units which could save them, and are sent home to die. This new fund will go towards the work of saving children – to intensive care units, transplant units, heart units, cancer units, whichever seem to be most urgently in need. Serving on the fund will be a leading paediatrician, as well as Debbie Hardwick, and Esther and Shaun. All the profits from this book will be donated by the BBC and by the authors, and by many bookshops, to the fund. We all hope that over the years more and more children will be saved, in Ben's name.

Transplant surgery is perhaps at the beginning of a long journey. There are the delicate problems of the surgery itself, the difficulties of tissue matching, and combating rejection. These difficulties are gradually being overcome, as new drugs and techniques are developed. Then there are the organisational problems – how to make sure that donors' organs and recipients reach each other as fast as possible. Desperately needed organs are surely lost at the moment, as hospitals can usually only work within the boundaries of their own areas. Transplant co-ordinators cannot contact intensive care units outside their own area health authority. That is why the *That's Life* office has sometimes been used as an unofficial matching unit, with consultants from hospitals in Scotland asking us what organs are needed, and hospitals in England appealing through us for organs to save a baby's life. There must be changes, to strengthen the network that exists through UK Transplant, so that a proper exchange of information, nationally, is achieved.

But most important of all, if the revolution Ben created is to continue and grow, more donors must come forward. Politicians believe there is an innate national prejudice against a system used in other countries of 'opting out' – under this system all of us would be regarded as potential donors, unless we have registered an objection. The *That's Life* MORI opinion poll showed that, given proper safeguards and if relatives are still consulted, 71 per cent of the nation is in favour of opting-out, and in fact prefer it to the donor card system. Perhaps in time an opt-out system will be adopted here, but until then, we can only hope that doctors and nurses have the courage to approach bereaved families, and the families themselves can respond with the kind of brave compassion we now know so well, from our viewers.

For if this story has taught us anything, we who work as television programme-makers, it is the strength of love and concern our viewers felt for Ben. His story has been criticised for being over-emotional, but when you tell the story of the people who fought for Ben's life, a story which described the triumph of love over death, then it must be emotional. The whole production team of the programme became involved, personally involved, with Ben's story.

We laughed with him, and we wept for him. To repeat the words one of our viewers wrote to Debbie and Billy, 'Everyone loved him – when he smiled he really did make the whole world smile with him. And the memory of Ben will never leave us.'

Among the bundles of letters we forwarded to Debbie Hardwick, one letter particularly impressed her. Attached to it was a newspaper cutting, faded and crumpled. None of us knows where it came from, or who composed it. It is the last will and testament of a donor, the kind of donor who saved the lives of so many of the people we have followed in this book. It contains the sentiments that inspired Rose Morrison, Julie and Darryl Fewkes, Kerry Ayliffe, and countless other donors whose names we will never know. Those are the people who have donated life, and this is their testament.

Remember Me

The day may come when my body will lie upon the white sheet in a hospital, busily occupied with the living and the dying. At a certain moment a doctor will determine that my brain has ceased to function, and that for all intents and purposes, my life has stopped.

When that happens, do not attempt to instil artificial life into my body by the use of a machine. And don't call this my deathbed. Let it be called the Bed of Life, and let my body be taken from it to help others lead fuller lives.

Give my sight to the man who has never seen the sun rise, a baby's face, or love in the eyes of a woman. Give my heart to a person whose own heart has caused nothing but endless days of pain. Give my blood to the teenager who was pulled from the wreckage of his car, so that he might live to see his grand-children play. Give my kidneys to the one who depends on a machine to exist. Take my bones, every muscle, every fibre and nerve in my body and find a way to make a crippled child walk.

Explore every corner of my brain. Take my cells, if necessary, and let them grow so that, some day, a speechless boy will shout, and a deaf girl will hear the sound of rain against her window.

Burn what is left of me and scatter the ashes to the winds to help the flowers grow. If you must bury something, let it be my faults, my weaknesses and all prejudice against my fellow man.

If, by chance, you wish to remember me, do it with a kind deed or word to someone who needs you. If you do all I have asked, I will live forever.

Ben died on Saturday, 23rd March 1985. But in the gifts of life he inspired, the love he engendered, his memory will live on.